WOMAN SHUT YOUR MOUTH!

Unmasking the myths and lies about women, submission, silence and subordination in religion and society.

BY FRANCESCA L. STUBBS

Forward By: Dr. Olive C. Brown

For information contact : www.sodaanmedia.com

Book and Cover design by
SODAAN PUBLISHING

A Subsidiary of

SODAAN Media & SODAAN GLOBAL INT'l.

P.O. Box 229 Spring Lake, NC 28390

ISBN-13 : 978 1724344915

ISBN-10 : 1724344919

First Edition: August 2018

© Francesca L. Stubbs 2018

10 9 8 7 6 5 4 3 2 1

Dedication

To my beautiful daughters, Jessica Michelle and Francesca Darnelle, who carry my legacy of womanhood and femininity for perpetuity; May you ever be proud of your womanhood and the fact that you are my daughters. All that I've survived and am becoming is for you! I love you beyond what my words can express. I declare over your life prosperity, wisdom in difficult situations and strength that overcomes every adversity that you may face. There is nothing you cannot accomplish. I am your proof and you are my reward! I am proud to call you my daughters.

To my one and only living sibling who shared the same womb as I, My Kimmie, and also to my dear cousin Jai; Our bond is unbreakable. Life has left us here together and I will always fight for you and be in your corner. May our inheritance of feminine grace, strength and resilience be imparted to those who follow after us. We are in this thing called life together and nothing will ever separate us.

To my Nieces: Charisa', Sharaya, Jahniece, Jatiah, TiaJanay, Da'Janae, Shawn, Angel, Anijah, Saleya Marie, Jaeda, Ava and cousin Chanel; May these words help you find your voice amidst the clamour of others and achieve all that your heart desires. No matter who says you can't, I believe in you and I say you CAN! So, dream it, do it, and do it big! Every hurdle our mothers have overcome has brought our dreams that much closer to achieving and no matter the adversity, Women, DON'T Shut Your Mouth!

CONTENTS

"My definition of sexism has been influenced by the way many social scientists in recent years have defined racism. That definition says that racism is an attitude, belief or practice that subordinates an individual or group on the basis of race. Thus, I define sexism as an attitude, belief or practice that subordinates an individual or group on the basis of sex." [gender]

Alvin John Schmidt

"Veiled and Silenced: How Culture Shaped Sexist Theology"

Introduction, xxvii

PREFACE

"Your silence will not protect you."

Audre Lorde

Writing this book has been a daunting task. Beginning to get this book together was an enormous undertaking. One of my greatest misgivings at the onset of this writing was the fact that I had so much information to sift through, so many experiences had -that could be included, and a certain desire to ensure that by thoroughly covering the subject matter, the intended target audience for this writing would be hit without any inadvertent occurrence of this sounding brash, condescending, or "man-hating." Being a woman and having to explain and/or prove that one knows what they are doing, and are worthy of and qualified for their current position has always been a difficult task; Especially when as a woman, it is quite common for one to be made to feel as though you must always scrape, scrounge or struggle, constantly being forced to prove who you are and that you possess "the goods". In church and secular society, there is the realization that this fight never ends. This book speaks to all of the above as well as to every woman who knows that God has called you to your post whether it be sacred or secular.

Maybe you have a business that you want to launch and begin working for yourself, but when you look around, it seems hard to continue or achieve the success that you long for. It may be that the circumstances which surround you constantly dictate whether or not you can be what you see yourself becoming. I want you to read each chapter. Take your time, go back and reread if you have to, and allow every word to sink in. You are not a second-class citizen! You are not God's backup plan! You are everything that God intended you to be from the day that you were created to this day. No, you're not perfect, but who's looking for perfection? You can be perfectly comfortable being who you are, with the gifts that you possess, the skills that you are proficient in and the beauty that you have from the inside out -and still be powerful, articulate and yes, full of grace. You don't have to dumb yourself down. You don't have to pin your hair up in a bun and walk around. Shame-faced because other people can't handle the power that you possess. You can be fully powerful, fully humble, fully a woman, fully YOU!

As we navigate through each chapter, it is completely recognizable that many women throughout history have had some very similar experiences. Again, I restate, this book is absent of the venomous bitterness, malice and "man-hating" unlike a great many texts that attempt to deal with this sensitive subject matter. The sole purpose is to serve as a resource that is uplifting, to speak life to every woman that has struggled or questioned herself - not because she was unsure of herself, but because she entered into the presence of others who were unsure of her power, abilities and expertise. It is their uncertainty, that somehow rubbed off and began to make her disbelieve in herself to the degree that she shut herself down and muted her Purpose all in a futile attempt to satisfy the insecurity of others.

Though we live in a country that is called "the land of the free, the home of the brave", it has been my experience that being a woman does not come with automatic privileges that guarantee any particular "liberty." In some cases, many women have felt that life may have been easier for them had they been born a man; What a ridiculous and terribly exaggerated thought!

You were created exactly as God intended; with everything in you that He fore-ordained you to have, He knew exactly what gender you needed to be as well as what you were placed here in the earth to do. It is my belief that your task and your gender are all interrelated. Your assignment in this life and your gender are both in perfect harmony and are synergistic with the plan of God. You see, you have to understand that your life would not be easier as another gender or in another body. It is not the physical that is in need of adjustment, but the mental and intellectual part of you that needs tweaking. If you are going to succeed in any arena, you must experience a paradigm shift in your mindset. It is my prayer that as you read, your thoughts are transformed to understand that though we live in a country that does not demand women wear veils as apparel, there are still veils unwittingly being placed upon women every day in the workplace, home, church and within other social structures in our society. These veils that many women have been forced to don are due in part or wholly to the insecurities of others who are intimidated by the very idea of a powerful woman. It is my prayer that as you read, every veil of perception, bondage, control and gender prejudice would fall off of you, knowing that just the way that you have been created in the body that you are in, you are full of power that needs no explanation. You don't have to make excuses for why you are the way you are or why you emote, the way you emote. You don't have to explain why you speak the way you speak. You don't have to create a reason for why you feel driven in the manner you do. I pray that upon completing the task of reading this book, you will see all of those things are intrinsically you, the woman God created you to be. Be comfortable in your own skin, being God's creation, walking in all of the power that is in you- powerfully woman, powerfully you!

You must learn to stop questioning when you have been given things that maybe others don't think that you deserve. You may have suffered. Yes, you may have gone through. You may have even had to endure lack and all kinds of ridicule, sarcasm and misunderstandings. You may have had many knives thrust in your back,. However, all of those things made you the woman that you are today.

As you read the following pages, be confident that what you have been created to do, you are already equipped to accomplish it. If it's launching a business, working in the corporate sector, being a mother, a wife, or a sister. If you are involved in ministry and you have a position in any capacity, know that you have already been totally equipped for the tasks at hand.

It is my prayer that this book would answer some pressing questions, help to calm your anxiety and sure-up your confidence in the fact that you are fearfully and wonderfully made- and not only so you are a powerful force to be reckoned with and God made you that way on purpose for purpose. So never again think you are God's backup plan or a just in case His first choice fails. You were always his first choice, even if you are not anyone else's..

FOREWORD

For decades there has existed an age-old discussion regarding the induction of women to ministry versus their obligatory submission to and support of their husbands as head. This often contentious dialogue, some believe, has occurred as a result of I Corinthians 14:34 (KJV) written by Apostle Paul, which reads; "Let your women keep silence in the churches: for it is not permitted unto them to speak; but they are commanded to be under obedience, as also saith the law." Historically, relationships between leaders have severed, reformations have split, and movements and even new denominations have formed on account of supposed divine revelation of the scripture.

Though I am appreciative of I Corinthians 14:34 because it is an integral part of the Word of God, in my research I have discovered that many leaders have taken key scriptural verses out of context, meaning they have proposed and disseminated revelation without first considering the entire book and chapter from which the particular verses are extracted. Regrettably, for this reason many women have held their love, worship, and desire to serve God in silence and, worst of all, determined not to heed and fulfill the purpose and call of God on their lives. I shudder to think of the countless people that could have been reached and significant work that could have been accomplished for the Kingdom of God had these women – married or unmarried – been released and made to feel free to answer the call of God. In studies I have discovered that as far back as 1893 women have served as senior leaders of churches. For example, the Presbyterian Church USA appointed its first female leader – Edith Livingston Peake – as Presbyterian Evangelist in San Francisco, California. During the 1940s, my introduction to the Church as a child, I observed women in senior leadership simultaneously serve their families and the Household of

Faith. Such women were high performing leaders, such as Bishop Ida Robinson, the Founder of Mount Sinai Holy Churches of America Incorporated headquartered in Philadelphia, Pennsylvania. This organization, Mount Sinai, received its charter from the State of Pennsylvania and began its work in 1923. Bishop Annie Chamblin, the Vice President of the Mount Sinai Holy Churches, established churches in Richmond, Virginia and Kinston, North Carolina, as well as initiated foreign missions in Port-Au Prince, Haiti. As her daughter, I shared her experiences in all of these cities, nationally and internationally.

A foundation of "order" was paramount as Mount Sinai was comprised of both male and female senior leaders, and Bishop Robinson, Bishop Chamblin, and numerous other women leaders were married and cared for their husbands, children, and homes in accordance with scripture and church policy. Women leaders were in subjection to their husbands and, at the same time, in subjection to the call of God on their lives. It is no wonder that these women's husbands fully supported them in ministry, simply because of their cordial demeanor and willingness to serve in the home. How can we silence or eliminate women from leadership of the church? Discussion of authority among men and women dates back as far as the biblical account of Adam and Eve, wherein according to Genesis 2:21, Eve was taken from the rib of Adam. Authority within the human race was established with Adam as the head and Eve positioned alongside him (i.e., the "rib", close to man's heart).

Today,…….. the woman also has powerful status as for nine months she carries, nourishes, protects, then births humanity. She contributes to the perpetuation of the human race, as Eve, the mother of all mankind.

With regards to 1 Corinthians 14, according to Halley (2007), "The discussion of the role of women in the church (vv.33-40) is a continuation of I Corinthians 11:2-16. Paul here forbids (vv.34-35) what he seems to allow in 11:5" (Halley, p. 709-710). Clarke (2018) explained, "'Let your women keep silence in the churches' was a Jewish ordinance; women were not permitted to teach in the assemblies, or even to ask questions. The rabbis taught 'woman should know nothing but the use of her distaff' (Clarke). Sayings of a familiar rabbi (Rabbi Eliezer, sec. 9, fol. 204) were, 'Let the words of the law be burned, rather than that they should be delivered to women…This was their condition till the time of the Gospel, when, according to the prediction of Joel, the Spirit of God was to be poured out on the women as well as the men, that they might prophesy (i.e. teach). And that they did prophesy or teach is evident from what the apostle says, 1 Corinthians 11:5, where he lays down rules to regulate this part of their conduct while ministering in the church" (Clarke). In consideration of the beliefs of the afore-mentioned scholars, I surmise that the background for I Corinthians 14:34 is there must have been some local circumstance or isolated event (unknown to us) that presented the need for and gave rise to the instructions – "possibly some bold women unbecomingly putting themselves forward"

(Halley). Again, I maintain that I deeply appreciate I Corinthians 14:34 – understood and observed in its full context of I Corinthians 14's discussion of the superiority of prophecy over tongues and order for use of gifts in the Church. Based on 50+ years in ministry under and now covering various dynamic leaders, I concur that some females (and even males, for that matter) can act unseemly in bold ostentatious demonstrations of gifts in the Church, however this is no cause to silence all of the women for the inappropriate behavior of a few. So, I say to all women: Advance and conquer for the Kingdom of God!

Finally, I esteem the great author of this book, Apostle Fran Stubbs, for painstaking research and untiring labor in writing this book, "Woman Shut Your Mouth". Her heart for the people of God, women in particular,- is evident in the pages of the book. Because we are living in a crucial time, we need men and women alike to heed the call and yield themselves to God – whether the purpose be in the churches, or on the city streets, byways, or in the home with family and friends. No work is insignificant in the eyes of the Lord. Remember Galatians 3:28 and 29 (Message Bible), which reads: "In Christ's family there can be no division into Jew and non-Jew, slave and free, male and female. Among us you are all equal. That is, we are all in a common relationship with Jesus Christ. Also, since you are Christ's family, then you are Abraham's famous 'descendant,' heirs according to the covenant promises."

Dr. Olive C. Brown
Presiding Prelate, International Christian Ministries

I Corinthians 14. Halley (2007). Halley's Bible Handbook with the New International Version, Deluxe Edition. Michigan: Zondervan.
1 Corinthians 14. Clarke (2018). Clarke's Commentary. Retrieved from biblehub.com/commentaries/ Clarke/1_corinthians/14.htm.

1

HER-STORY

During my early life, circumstances were difficult. I grew up rough, for lack of a better term. My mother died when I was a teenager and I felt as though I was left to fend in life alone. I didn't really know my father as a young child. So as a result, when my mother passed away, I lived here and there until finally there was a point where one of my sisters and myself went to live with my father. Life with our father was not easy. You see, he wasn't accustomed to fulltime fatherhood for any of his children, not to mention two teenage daughters. Because of this, he didn't know how to handle issues that teen girls deal with — and add to the fact that we were all still grieving the loss of our mother, well, it wasn't pretty. Long story short, we didn't stay there. We ran away from home after being with him several months and were back once again to moving from pillar to post. Many things happened along that journey. I was mistreated, raped and molested by people who were supposed to be caregivers. These are just details that added to the tragedy that was my life at that time. However, that's not what this story is about. I must admit that those terrible events taught me to fight and persevere though difficulty. No matter how bad things were, I still learned so much about life and it helped me to become the woman that I am today. We are all a product of our experiences. The good and the bad. Everything that we have endured has taught us invaluable lessons and has shaped us in some way. Life continued to progress, even though it didn't seem much like progress, however in some small way, it was.

One afternoon, I heard someone sharing a message of the gospel of Jesus Christ as I was riding on the train. As I was listening, I just knew that this person was speaking directly to me. My life was already in shambles. The things that I had or that I thought I had didn't bring me peace. I was caught up in a lifestyle of alcohol, drugs and illicit sex. I was drinking liquor almost daily, and smoking and snorting cocaine whenever I could get my hands on it. I did so many shameful things and it was ravaging my life. I was unhappy because of the great loss that I suffered by the death of my mother, which I came to understand, had such a tremendously negative impact upon my life. The effect was so great that I didn't really understand how earth shattering it was until I became an adult and looked back over my life with wonder and amazement that I made it to adulthood. Losing all that you have, has a way of shaping you as an individual. It has a way of marring your perception of life, what happiness is supposed to look like, and what your expectations should be. Many of us have suffered earth shattering experiences and somehow, we seem to pick up the pieces and keep going. You know the old adage, "you never know how strong you are until you have to be strong"? Well, I learned that early on. There's no such thing as "I quit." There's no such thing as "I give up", even though I have tried to do so many times. Those years as a young girl growing up without having that strong woman figure, having a mother's love and nurturing hand to guide my life, did more damage than I could put into words at that time. Losing someone who was so influential and who knew better than myself, took an enormous toll upon me. I was devastated. I didn't have anyone to help me through life's battles. I didn't have anyone to show me how to take courage as I navigated from teenager to womanhood, from child to parent. I so needed and longed for her voice, her influence and her love.

This is just a part of life, I thought. It was my life. I didn't have anyone to say the things that every young woman needs to hear coming from her mother as she is transitioning through life. Not having that, I learned to mother myself. I learned to be my own comfort, and my own help. Somehow, I figured out how to be strong and say all the things to myself that I thought my mother would tell me if she were still here. This is my life as I know it and then this message of Jesus hits me like a ton of bricks! When I heard that message, it was transformational for me. I froze in my seat, listening to the preacher and his message. Even though I was the quintessential heathen, I knew exactly what he was talking about when he was preaching and sharing the Gospel. There was no doubt in my mind and I understood completely that his message meant that I needed salvation. That very day, I set out to make salvation a reality in my life. I found the nearest place that I thought I would find someone to talk to me, I went into a Christian bookstore and began to talk to one of the individuals who worked there.

It was to my joy, that I discovered upon sharing my plight, that I happened to be speaking with an individual who had endured some of the same things that I had endured. What a relief to know that what I had gone through was not so unique that it was unheard of. It Wasn't some anomaly, but these things had occurred to her as well. After sharing my situation, The young lady at the bookstore began to share the gospel and led me to Christ. All I can say is, when I lifted my hands and I prayed that prayer for salvation and repentance, I meant it with all my heart. I remember after I prayed, in rushed a flood of peace like I have never known. It was something that I had not had before. I don't even have words to describe it, but from that day on I was changed. Hence, this was the beginning of my journey of how I got here.

Living for Christ was everything to me. Even today this sentiment rings true. I know that some who are educated say that religion is for the weak, that it's a crutch. However, these are people who are completely oblivious to the fact that we were created for God's glory and not only that, there's only so much that the human psyche can endure before it loses its homeostasis and suffers a breakdown. There's only so much that we can bear on our own as humans. It is a wise man who understands that he needs a God who is able to feel our infirmities and show us the way to endure. Now that I had become a "Believer"' I had that in my relationship with Jesus. How glad I was about this new relationship, having escaped the torment I was in previously.

This new life meant everything to me and as time progressed, I begin to attend a church and grow in my faith. Things in my life began to change. The things that I had perceived, and thought I had wanted previously, I acknowledged that those were no longer my desires. I did, however want a family, I wanted to be a wife. Why? Because I had lost the sense of family with the death of my mother, so this was always a great longing that I had inside. I just wanted to have a family. I wanted to be able to have children that I could love and that would love me back. I wanted to have a husband that I could love and who would love me in return. Those were my greatest prayer requests. Eventually the Lord didn't answer my prayer. Oh, how happy I was. That's a long story in and of itself, but I was overjoyed at the answer to my prayers. Finally, I would have my own family and be the mother to my children that I so longed to have in my own life.

1989 was a great year! It was a year filled with many transitions, but it was still a great year. In the midst of all that was going on in life, I got married. My husband had enlisted as a soldier in the United States Army. I wasn't too enthused about that because I was afraid of moving away from home and what could happen to him in the event our country should go to war. I still don't understand my apprehension concerning moving away from what I called home-whatever home was because I really didn't really have a home. However, I was excited about the prospect of seeing a different place with the man I was to marry. I just wasn't ready for everything that was ahead and as a young woman, a newly married young married woman, not really having a mother to teach you what marriage was, set me up for many situations for which I was ill-prepared. What was the expectation my husband had of me as his wife? How could I be a good wife? What are a wife's responsibilities? You know, you look to the church for that interpretation and the interpretation that I received was not quite biblical. It was quite oppressive to be honest. It was the old antiquated "wives be submitted to your husband's mentality" which we know comes from the scripture, However, misunderstood and misconstrued it might have been.

It was for me, a culture shock because in light of the fact that where I had come from and the life that I had lived and survived, the definitions of a godly wife and having a family that were presented left much to be desired. How do you take a survivor and a fighter who's had to fight hard to live through so much trauma that she now has to learn to follow every instruction that comes from her spouse, and do so obediently and with respect? How do you teach Someone who has never really had anyone to look out for her, or that she could rely on how to submit as a wife, and allow her husband to rule her because he is now her head? I had a gigantic problem coming to terms with these things. Now I had to follow someone else's instructions, for EVERYTHING! Say what? Do what? I wasn't sure how that was going to work out, and it didn't work well. Needless to say, the beginning of our marriage was quite rocky, and that's an understatement. Because I came from this background of always having to fight, always having to make a way for myself, and now I'm in a place where I'm married to someone who feels as though their job is to love and take care of me. Not only so, but I found it somewhat troublesome that these so-called biblical definitions of being a wife also included but were not limited to my allowing someone to lead me, tell what I could and couldn't do, as well as having parameters placed upon me that dictated how much liberty I had. but wait a minute, did not ask God for this? Isn't this the answer to my prayer? That's what I thought. So the battle ensued. What was the battle you might ask? The battle was for me to submit. Now I'm going to deal with that later on in another chapter, but I need to make it plain because I'm sure that there are several women that are reading this right now who can identify with the fact that in the church we have been told, submit, submit, submit, but often it is presented in an unbiblical manner. Now for some of us who are of the African American persuasion, I am sure that you can identify with the fact that one of the first verses that some of the men in our churches learn and memorize is, "wives submit yourselves to own husbands."[1] Yes, I'm quite familiar with this as well. I'm sure that you can identify with the feelings that I felt as well. I was always feeling like I was being suffocated. It was as if someone was putting a muzzle on me, shutting me down from all that I was. Now mind you, I don't believe that all of the fighting and the struggle to survive the environments that I had grown up in should've been projected into my marriage relationship. Admittedly that was partially the culprit of many of our early difficulties. However, when you learn something all your life, it's hard to let it go.

How do I reconcile who I was with this new person that I should be now? Shouldn't I be able to just put my guard down instantly because now my prayers have been answered? I have the man that I wanted. He loves me. I love him. We're going to be a happy family. Shouldn't I be relaxed now? That was the hard part. That was just part of the difficulty I was experiencing. On top of that, I needed healing. On top of that, I needed to be able to embrace my womanhood and know that there was nothing intrinsically wrong with me being frank, strong, or just being "Fran". It was perfectly fine to be "Fran"- a woman who wants to accomplish things. There is nothing bad about being the "Fran" who wants to be great, because God wanted me to be creative, but at the same time I needed to know how to balance all of those things because part of my greatness included being a wife. A huge part of my greatness included being a super mom with great children and living this fantasy life - because that's exactly what it was. In the beginning, everything was a fantasy. I fantasize about everything being perfect. I've fantasized about there not being any arguments, disagreements and us being one big happy family. It wasn't until some time had passed that I realized that I had begun to turn the volume down on my life. I begin to shut myself down because I didn't fit the quintessential submitted wife role. I began to compare myself to other women that I saw who were wives, and I figured, well, if that's what I'm supposed to be, I guess I need to change my ways so that I can measure up and be like these other wives. I started to practice being quiet. I thought of ways to hold my peace. I focused solely on cleaning the house, washing the clothes, cooking meals, raising the children, and doing everything in my power to make my husband happy. I wanted to satisfy his definition of a wife. Be "Fran" but just do it quietly.

I was a mess! As I look at the scripture, how Sarah called Abraham Lord[2], I began to think, that my husband was my lord and I was to submit to him and I was to be quiet. How do I do that? Everything about my life was loud! My mouth was loud, my thoughts were loud. Just being "Fran" in general. Loud. I'm a New York girl and not very many of us New York women are quiet. We grow up yelling up the street. We call our friends by hollering out the window. This is what we do. It's our culture. How do I turn the volume on that down? Now mind you, I'm very lady like, but I can be very loud and bring all of my New York out just as well. I was trying to learn how to turn myself down. I wanted to turn down my driven personality that loves to pursue and be a "go-getter." I began to realize how difficult it was to be myself and what my husband, pastor and even what I understood at the time the Bible was commanding me to be. It was beyond difficult. It was so difficult that I wasn't sure our marriage wouldn't buckle under the pressure of this issue.

Today, my husband and I have come to be on good terms about where I stand in the faith. We argued about my submission because it was so hard for me. Then again, we would go to church and I would hear pastor preach and he would talk about how the wives were supposed to behave themselves and the pastor's wife would reiterate more of the same during women's meetings. There I was, saying to myself, how do I do this? Does that mean that I can't have any aspirations? Does that mean that I can't go after anything? Does that mean that I have no voice? What does submission mean? What does it mean for my house? What does it mean for all the things that I know that God has put in my heart to do? How can I possibly do those things and still be submitted? What if my husband doesn't want me to do them? What if he disagrees? What if he feels like I'm not supposed to do anything outside of being his wife and supporting him? That's where the difficulties entered in.

Fast forward several years and I had to deal with the changing of some theology. That's a whole different story by itself. Suffice it to say, I've had to make adjustments having a spouse that does not believe that women should preach, or that women should have leadership positions within the church outside of leading other women. Yes, you can teach in schools, you can do Sunday school for the women and for the children, but never over men. No, you cannot have an authoritative role over men in church. How do I pursue what I know I'm supposed to be pursuing when the one that I love does not agree? We'll deal with that later, but I will admit that I had to work through many difficulties, hardships, make many adjustments personally, for my business as well as ministry. I have suffered humiliation in front of others, having to hold my head up when I felt like I shouldn't be holding my head down for shame. I have cried myself to sleep many nights praying for change while watching my family split apart, and then come back together. I have had to deal with the angst of a promise that I received from the Lord, not knowing when it's ever going to come to pass. All the while holding on to my faith and attempting to be faithful doing what I knew to do was right.

Seriously, how did I get here? That's a long story whose ending I'm still writing even as this book is going into publication. Whatever it is that you face, whatever it is that you feel that God has called you to do, we all know that our stories have a beginning. But one thing that we all can rejoice about is that there's also an ending- even if it seems that it is nowhere in sight. And it is by faith that we believe and know that our ending is going to be good. We just have to endure through all of the parts in between.

2

TRADITION OR SCRIPTURE

"Be a first- rate version of yourself, not a second-rate version of someone else."

~Judy Garland~

In this particular chapter, we will deal with traditional versus biblical ideologies concerning wives (women) keeping silent. I would like to share a quote from the book, "Me, Obey Him? By Elizabeth. Rice -Hanford. This text shares a very traditional, almost ultra-traditional viewpoint regarding womanhood, and the subjection of women to their husbands. There's no exegetical work being done on the verses from 2nd Timothy 2:11,12 - which is the basis of this book in Mrs. Hanford's mindset.

She quotes the following: "There are many other scriptures concerning obedience to authority, specifically these tell a wife to obey her husband, but before we go any further, let's consider regardless of your idea of what these scriptures mean, can we agree that they all say, wives should obey her husband beyond a shadow of a doubt. The scriptures say, a woman ought to obey her husband! Why not reread each verse, answering these questions:

Is there, in any one of them, a restriction on a wife's obedience? Does a single Scripture mention any situation were a wife ought not to obey? Is any command qualified by any "if"? If the husband were not a Christian. If the wife thought God were leading her contrary to her husband? Is there a hint

that a wife may choose between conflicting authorities? If you
are intellectually honest, you have to admit that it is impossible
to find a single loophole, a single exception, and "if" or
"unless." The Scriptures say, without qualification, to the
open-minded reader, that a woman ought to obey her
husband."[1]

Is this an unequivocal statement? If I were to spin her questions around, Shouldn't we reread each verse within "its given context" to get an understanding? To answer these questions, we must first decide what situations could arise that would place, a restriction on a wife's obedience? Does a single scripture referenced in the above -mentioned author's book take into account any situation where a wife ought not to obey? What if the husband is not a Christian and prohibits his wife from any/all church attendance? Why wouldn't the wife be able to follow God if He truly is leading her contrary to her husband's command? Is there a hint in any scripture that indicates that a wife doesn't have the ability/power to choose between conflicting authorities? If you really are intellectually honest, Which I do not believe Mrs. Hanford is truthfully expecting the reader to be, you must admit that it is indeed possible to find more than a single loophole and exception based upon the proper interpretation. We can, with proper exegesis prove that the scriptures say without question, to the open -minded reader and closed minded alike, that a woman is not commanded to obey in the context that the author is intending to convey. This is where I would like to insert my address to these traditional, unbiblical doctrines. The author quoted above is indeed someone who has been taught the scripture from an eisegetical point of view versus exegetical. In this particular chapter of her book, which is entitled: "What do the scriptures say about a wife's obedience?," She makes several unbiblical claims without properly presenting historic fact with her interpretations. It is this mindset that must be dealt with and truth must be introduced to those who desire the truth and want to be released from the bondage of false teaching.

She quotes specifically from several verses of scripture and does not provide any proofs to support her interpretation for them. What is missing is the historicity, culture, and the exegetical meaning. She extrapolates her beliefs about submission from Genesis 3:16 which says, "Unto the woman, God said, thy desire shall be to the husband and he shall rule over thee." She quotes also from Ephesians 5:22, in which Paul states, "wives, submit yourselves to your own husbands as unto the Lord;" and finally, from the living letters paraphrase, which says, "Submit to your husband's leadership in the same way you submit to the Lord." This is problematic for several reasons, but specifically, one cannot interpret verses from Ephesians 5:22 about wives submitting to their husbands without first reading the verses which precede the text in question. The pretext speaks specifically for us (all Believers), to submit one to another. It is clear that though Mrs. Hanford is zealous and has articulately laid the foundation for her doctrinal statements, it is apparent that her foundation is faulty in its conclusions. It is unfortunate that the text presented lacks in understanding the mutuality that is being conveyed by the Apostle Paul's writings.

Like so many others who affirm this traditional interpretation, Elizabeth Hanford presents an all or nothing set of rules that lock women into an archaic mindset of servitude and subordination to men. This is done, all the while using misinterpretations of Scriptures as proof of accuracy. This presents much difficulty for those who study the Scripture thoroughly and have found the true meaning of what Paul intended in his statements to the new Believers concerning marital life and the roles individuals should assume. Mrs. Hanford also takes a crack at the following verse from Colossians 3:18 which says, "Wives, submit yourselves unto your own husbands as it is in the Lord." And then she also quotes from the The Living Letters Paraphrase of the same verse which says, "You wives, submit yourselves to your husbands for that is what the Lord has planned for you." Also, she shares from the Williams translation, which says, "For this is your Christian duty." (The footnote says "literally - fitting in the Lord that is - it is proper, or as it befits a Christian.") So, as we see here, there are several verses that pertain to the subject of wives, submission and their behavior- all of which we see have been taken out of context. I would insert this one caveat for anyone who is reading this - if you accept the traditional ideology without understanding the historical and cultural issues that impacted the people in that region and era, you will also neglect mounds of necessary information that played a significant role in the assertion of Paul's doctrinal position. It is also unwise to take one blurb or even several verses out of context and posit those verses as doctrinal truth- teaching others to believe that women are to be silent.

The one thing that is somewhat amusing to me, and I don't mean this in a disrespectful manner, however, is   in the block quote above where Elizabeth is speaking, she actually makes an allusion to being intellectually honest. As you read her interpretation of scripture, it is fair to assert that there is no true intellectual benefit to those who thoroughly study the Scripture. It is evident the process she has taken in interpreting the scripture is one of taking the writings at face value and literal. It is clear she has not taken the time to use exegesis to develop her theories, as others who believe the same do. We are commanded to "Study to show ourselves approved unto God, a workman that need not be ashamed rightly dividing the word of truth."(2 Tim. 2:15) We see that she has neglected to rightly divide the word. This is not a pun against her abilities or even disrespectful. However, in making these assumptions and drawing conclusions on what it is that we believe, we must be honest when we encounter these versions of scripture that fail to properly and rightly divide the Word. She even goes so far in this particular chapter of this book to make reference to women obeying their husbands without any feeling about what the will of God is.[2]

How can we possibly make an assumption that the will of God would include our silence when Jesus himself gave rise to women speaking? Jesus himself who lifted women, in his contact with them showed those around Him God's heart towards women. Jesus gave women permission, even authority to carry his message. There is no mention of this "new pattern" set by Christ in her book. She speaks about how a woman should handle things if she feels that God is speaking to her to do one thing or she feels "lead" to do something that her husband disagrees about. Her answer is to forget the urge to walk contrary to your husband and follow his instructions- unequivocally and without reservation, no matter what! There is no correct scriptural basis for these things. However, she argues that the afore-mentioned scriptures say that a woman should ignore her feelings about whatever she feels the will of God is and that she should obey her husband because that is the highest law. Now that's lunacy! (In my opinion.) She even goes so far as to say that the man that you are married to takes the place of God and is the voice of God in your life.[3]

If we have the spirit of God on the inside and if God wanted us to be silent, just ask yourself if any of the above teachings make "intellectual or spiritual sense" to you? The scripture tells us, and we have spoken of this already in this book, that the spirit of God is given to every man to profit withal.[4] Man is not Holy Spirit. When you read this verse of Scripture, it is talking about the fact that the Spirit of God has given to every individual who is a believer without discrimination. It doesn't matter if they are male or female. So, to take this verse and misinterpret it or in this case – disregard it altogether, is shameful. There is no portion of the Word of God that teaches that man (husband) becomes the voice of God to his wife. The spirit of God has been given to every man (woman) to profit withal, meaning, it is for our benefit (every Believer) that the Spirit of God has been given each of us. Including us women.

In this chapter. She also uses a verse of scripture that I have used and stood on; but I believe that she has also taken it out of context. She mentions Numbers

30:6-16; These verses speak of a woman who has vowed a vow to the Lord and her husband is not aware of it. When the wife makes the vow and her husband is not privy to it, God forgives her of the vow because he stands over her in authority. We know that this is an old testament practice and old testament law. Understanding the time in which this is written aids in our comprehension of how things were done. I have quoted this verse as it pertains to women fasting or when there are times where wives may have set aside time to pray and seek the Lord without the knowledge or mutual agreement between she and her husband. In a case such as this, it becomes something that you can be released from because of your marital agreement. It does not mean that you are absolved from every commitment you made to the Lord just because you are married. Mrs. Hanford paints a picture of a woman who has no relationship with the Lord aside from that which comes through her Husband. This is false teaching. Paul deals with this subject in the Epistles and addresses the covenant of marriage and states that BOTH husband AND wife should not neglect one another because of fasting and prayer without MUTUAL CONSENT. (1Corinthians 7:5-6). Again, this is the idea of mutuality and one ruling over the other.

Every chapter within this book that I am referencing at this point is replete with "traditional" and erroneous ideologies. These doctrines have been taught for centuries in the church and has kept women in bondage for years within their marriages, their ministries and within society. It behooves us to make sure that we study and receive correct and thorough knowledge of the Word of God, especially if we are going to teach it to others. A good rule of thumb to consider is: "text out of context is no text at all." If a verse has been made the basis for a doctrine by extrapolating it from the text- but the doctrine makes no sense within the given context of the entire chapter, that doctrine must be rejected, denied and discarded- for it is heresy! It is unfortunate that this book -and others like it, is used or has been used as a tool to keep women in line so to speak, within their marriages. Presupposing a book about marital relationships and the way husbands and wives connect and function within their covenant seems to be a good idea. Every couple longs for a healthy marriage. But the question must be addressed as to how a woman may fulfill the call of God if she is married yet repressed because of inaccurate dogma?

It is impossible. In plain language, God is not repressing women, married or single alike. The things that we have previously thought must be challenged and held under the scrutiny of the word of God. His word is true. Even though we live in a secular society, it is understood that these ideologies have permeated our culture throughout centuries and is a major reason why these teachings are still pervasive today. I would like to add that my difficulty with Elizabeth Rice Hanford's book is the fact that this book totally disregards the personhood of each woman who reads, whether she is a wife or single. The reality is that in her book, she addresses women in such a manner in which she has no voice. That woman becomes invisible. That is the mentality that is gathered as you read her book. It is as if women though you are valuable, your highest value comes through being a wife and that you have no voice and that the life, the mind and the authority of your husband overshadows the rights, life, and the opinions that you would have as an individual. In my opinion, this is because her treatment is so harsh and her wording and verbiage is so strong that it becomes very apparent that her point cannot be missed.

She even has a chapter entitled "Don't I have any rights?" She misconstrues the scripture about being submitted to the will of God as being quietly submitted without argument, or without rebuttal to one's husband. Some of her teachings about what our rights and privileges are as believers is correct. However, it is misinterpreted as all rights being given over to your husband. It is almost as if she is putting chains on wives and saying that this is a part of your walk of faith. Her message conveys that it is by faith that you submit and God will give you the grace and ability necessary to hold yourself down and lock away all of your ambition for life. Along with your zeal and fervor so that you will be able to be happy with just being a wife who is submitted to what is given to you by your husband.

She talks about how it is such a relief to be free from having to make any decisions. She writes about the fact that you (the wife,) should be relieved because now you'll have someone who is concerned about your lifelong welfare and the things that are pertaining to you. And so since it's her job to submit, it is his job to be responsible for all other matters in life for you. She teaches that wives should be happy because they are basically footloose and fancy free. That is the most ludicrous idea I have ever heard! It is almost as if one is to believe that since they are bound by the contract of marriage, nothing else in life should affect them (the wife) because she has no responsibility except to her husband. Everything else pertaining to her is his responsibility.

She's not responsible to make any decisions. She's not responsible to a wake up in the morning and make any choices about her life and needs. All of those things are brought under the submission of her husband and therefore she (the wife,) becomes a willing servant. It really doesn't sound like a marriage at all. It Sounds like slavery! I think it is very important to know the truth. This is why though I've had this book and many like it on my shelf for years-I couldn't bring myself to accept what I was reading. I, like many people, wanted to be this perfect wife. I knew that what I had read could not possibly be God's mindset. Now mind you, I don't want anyone to think that what I'm saying that as a wife, you should just run loose and do whatever it is that you want to do, without concern, love or respect for your husband's opinion. However, what I am saying is that we're not chained to a radiator. God is not stripping wives of their ability to make choices; Nor is he stealing your freedom from you as an individual so that you cannot make any choices. God's Word does not teach that you don't have to do anything in life, but just lived under the control of someone making decisions for you, because you are married.

As I said, when you read her book, she uses very strong language, much of which is her opinion and doctrinal beliefs versus what scripture actually means, Therefore, it is very important that anyone who ascribes to this particular belief system - studies to make sure that what is believed is actually biblical and not just traditional teachings of men. I'm sure that my words are strong language as well. For some who may not believe in what is being expressed as Biblical ideology within the pages of this book. The problem is, many people still ascribe to the traditional ideology even when they know it's extrabiblical. Some people believe, yes, women can preach, women can start a business, women can run a fortune 500 company, but when it comes to marriage, there's no mutuality- this is the place that women must be in submission to her husband, no if's and's or but's. This kind of teaching is error and it is unbiblical, whether we like it or not.

Submission is due benevolence to one another, kindness. Many take due benevolence to mean something sexual and it's not always something sexual. It can be, of course in the context of marriage, but when we are speaking of due benevolence as the scripture does, it is showing kindness to one another, it is doing things that exemplify the love, the life and the character of Christ by putting others person first. That is the requirement for all of us as Believers. The requirement is no different as husband and wife.

3

IS THAT BIBLE?

"What is the greatest lesson a woman should learn? That since day one, she's already had everything she needs within herself. It's the world that convinced her she did not."

~Rupi Kaur~

This brings me to my next point of addressing the traditional teachings concerning women in marriage, I would like to also deal with Genesis 3:16. The Bible says, "And your desire shall be for your husband." This is after Adam and eve had sinned and because of their sin, there was a curse placed upon both Adam and eve. They both had to pay a consequence for the choice to disobey God. I would like to deal with this verse of scripture because this is another one of those verses that is most famously used when many teach about women being submitted to their husbands and what God's will is. It seems to be forgotten that this verse is after they sin and a curse is placed upon them for their rebellion against God's command. Somehow, we forget that Jesus has come to free us from the curse of the law of sin and death. The work of the cross took care of the curse. These facts must be stated before can address the state and standing of mankind. It is taught that the result of the curse still lingers on the woman and this verse is used as an argument to posit women as Jezebels and rebellious. We know that the Bible tells us that we've been made free from the law, and from the curse of the law of sin and death. However, we do not always apply it as we should. So let's look more carefully at this verse. It says, "to the woman, he said, I will surely multiply your pain in childbearing. In pain. You shall bring forth children, your desire shall be for your husband and he shall rule over you." Genesis 3:16. Let's break down this verse. What do these words mean? "Your desire shall be for your husband." This is going to be a two-fold explanation. I want to expound on this because some people think that this word, Teshuqah- which is the Hebrew word for desire, that is used here in Genesis 3:16, simply means a desire such as a longing or a want. It is often misconstrued and defined as a desire in the sense of women fighting for power to rule over her husbands. I want to break a few things down to provide clarity for this verse and to remove any false understanding about what this really means. I would also advise that in your free time, after you have read this, that you will actually go further research this word.

In chapter Fifteen of Gloria Cotton's book, " In The Beginning: Restoring God's Vision for Woman," She writes about facing the consequences of the first man and woman - Adam and Eve, sinning; The result of sin in the life of women and how it manifests, and in her estimation, when the Scripture says, "your desires shall be for your husband," Her thoughts are as follows:

> "The first and most obvious meaning concerns sexual attraction. Eve, says God, will have sexual desire for her husband. This desire will not diminish even though their union will result in pregnancy and the painful labor of childbirth. Before she sinned, sexual desire for her husband had been a source of joy and unadulterated pleasure. The possibility of conception, before the advent of sin, only enhanced the intimacy of marriage. Now that childbirth would bring intense pain, thoughts of conception would be tainted with fear, and marital intimacy with sometimes suffer as a result. Regardless of her fear, Genesis 3:16 tells us she will be at the mercy of the stronger man who "...shall rule over her." The man's sexual appetite and his desire for children will overrule her fears because he will have enough strength to dominate her. In addition, the woman would be driven by sexual lust and by dependence upon the man for the satisfying of our sexual appetites. Before sin entered their relationship, the focus on each spouse had been upon loving and blessing the other. For both husband and wife, love for one another had found expression in marital intimacy. However, now that sin has tainted their relationship, the noble submission of the woman is reduced to subservience, and the virtuous headship of the man is debased to dominance as each becomes focused on his own need. The beautiful gift of oneness that God designed for marriage degenerates into two people seeking to get their needs met, each causing his sexuality to appease his own desires.

The Hebrew word translated husband in this verse is the Hebrew "ish," meaning man, any man, all men or husband. It is used hundreds of times in the Old Testament and is translated in all of these ways. Consequently, the indication is, that because of sin, even her daughters will have sexual desire for men in general. Sexuality as created by that was pristine in its purity and exclusive and it's focused upon one husband. But sin turned that into giving, nurturing, loving sexuality into a self-centered appetite that knows no loyalty. Lust has been born in the hearts of Eve and will be inherited by her daughter's. However, the rebellious nature now birth in her through her sin, produces in Eve not only sexual frustration, but also a host of unmet emotional needs in her life. She was created for a relationship, but the primary relationship of her life, her marriage with Adam is broken. Her built in the to give and receive affection to share her life intimately at all levels is unmet.

As a result, she and her daughters become bottomless pits for love and attention. This painful emotional vacuum can only be filled by God. but her relationship with him is broken also. Therefore, the tendency of Eve and our daughters is to look to men, not only to fulfill their sexual desires, but also to meet their emotional needs as well. Women who follow this natural tendency become vulnerable to men, especially men who are domineering. Even when these women managed to find a relationship with a kind and gentle man, no matter how much love and attention he gives, he can never fill the bottomless pit in her soul."[1]

So that's just one woman's understanding of this verse in Genesis. I partially agree with her statement as it relates to the relationship troubles that many women have and the black hole of unmet needs. As I have stated, I can only agree with this statement partially.

I would like to share another quote to assist in providing understanding and then I will share in my own words my thoughts about what the Hebrew word Teshuqah (desire) actually means. This is an appropriate segway to address what I meant about the woman filling a black hole in her relationships. The best way to provide a proper explanation is to build upon the definition of the word "desire" used in the verse in question, as explained from the Liddel -Scott-Jones

Lexicon of ancient Greek. The purpose of using a Greek lexicon is due to the fact that the Old Testament was translated from the Greek- as the Septuagint (LXX) is a Greek document. Therefore, the word Teshuqah is translated as "apostrophe". There are several meanings given in the aforementioned lexicon for this word, but in the context of Gen 3, the definition that makes the most sense is definition #3: Apostrophe means turning away from all others to one person;[2]. We are in a time that this word is most absolutely correct. If we look at our lives, and how we have governed ourselves, if we as women would make a true assessment of how we have carried on in our relationships; The real truth is that this word, as described above- this curse that is spoken of in Genesis 3 of a certainty means that we would put husbands in the place of God in our life- and this thing ought not to be so.

Remember I quoted to you from Mrs. Hanford's book, "Me, Obey Him?", Where her ideology and traditional view of women is that man or the husband becomes the voice of God for the wife instead of her being able to rely on Holy Spirit? That is the purpose of Holy Spirit in our lives; "to lead and guide us into all truth".[3] To posit a man in that place, any man, it is blatant error and those who follow such teachings, trust a theology that cannot hold water. The so-called struggle, the power struggle is not that a woman will try to rule over the husband. I disagree that her desire is for his place as a man. Though that may be the case for some, my argument is that this purported struggle for supremacy and to rule over the man is not the correct understanding of the text presented. Based upon my studies and the proof presented in the form erroneous present-day theological doctrine, along with the definition provided in the previous paragraph, I submit to you that the true curse is the struggle to keep God as God in your life and not allowing a man to take that place! The result of the "Curse" is, IDOLATRY! Turning to the affection of your husband or a man at times when your heart should be turning to God- this is what is being spoken of in Genesis chapter 3. The fight to worship God and Him only continues in the heart today.

With full knowledge of God's command, Eve disobeyed- knowing the direct order that came from God, that they should not touch that tree nor eat the fruit of it- she sinned and ate. Her response? Instead of going to God after she had been tempted, she turned to her husband and gave it to him as well. She looked to her husband when she sinned instead of turning to God with repentance and brought Adam with her into sin. I submit to you that it is a sinful act for a woman to go to her husband instead of turning to God when she has a void that needs to be filled inside-that only God can meet. It is an ungodly act to put more trust in the man you marry then in the God who created you. Whenever we put anyone in a place in our heart that they should not have, we set ourselves up for them to become idols to us. This is what the warning is declaring in the text. This is the curse that is spoken of in genesis 3:16. It is a warning that marriage for some women would become idolatrous in that they would put their husbands before everything including their relationships with God. When you look at it from this vantage point, this is a powerful thought. After taking the time to study and break down this word, when you look at how much sense this makes this eye-opening. Therefore, when we read genesis 3:16, we must read it as a warning that we would always keep God first. That he would always have preeminence in our life. That is biblical theology. When we properly understand the Word of God, we understand our place as women and in the body of Christ.

Below, is a quote from Marg Mowczko's blog entitled. *"The Woman's 'Desire' In Genesis 3:19."* She shares a more indepth explanation of the word Teshuqah as used in Genesis 3. It is of utmost importance that ample study is given to this word and that we not take a light perusing of this subject as doctrinal truth is necessary if we are to obey the commands of Scripture and avoid error.

TESHUQAH: A RARE WORD

Several words that are crucial in understanding what the Bible shows us about the relationship between men and women are rare and somewhat obscure in their original languages. I've previously written about the Hebrew word kenegdo which occurs only twice in the Old Testament (in Genesis 2:18 and 20). And I've looked at the Greek word authentein which occurs only once in the New Testament (in 1 Timothy 2:12). In this post I look at the Hebrew word teshuqah in Genesis 3:16. This word also occurs in Genesis 4:7 and Song of Solomon 7:10. Three times in all.

In Genesis 3:16 God says to the woman: "I will greatly multiply Your pain in childbirth, In pain you will bring forth children; Yet your desire (teshuqah) will be for your husband, And he will rule over you." NASB Until Susan Foh wrote her 1974-5 paper What is a Woman's Desire?, many Bible translators were content to understand teshuqah as simply meaning "desire" and "longing".[1] A few English translations such as the NLT and NET, however, show the influence of Foh's paper. They have translated teshuqah as "desire to control" and "want to control" in Genesis 3:16. Is "a desire to control" what the original authors meant in Genesis and in Song of Solomon?

TESHUQAH IN HEBREW LEXICONS

In the Brown-Driver-Briggs Hebrew Lexicon (BDB) it says that teshuqah means "longing": a longing of woman for man in Genesis 3:16; a longing of man for woman in Song of Solomon 7:11;[2] and, figuratively, a longing of a beast (representing sin) to devour Cain in Genesis 4:7.[3] Furthermore, BDB claims that teshuqah is derived from a stem shuq which means "attract, impel, of desire, affection".[4] Gesenius likewise states that teshuqah is derived from the stem shuq which has the meanings "to run after, to desire, to long for anything; whence תְּשׁוּקָה [teshuqah means] desire, longing."[5] Other lexicons, such as HALOT, also define teshuqah as "desire, longing." None of these lexicons, however, connect teshuqah with a desire to control. [OBJ] Screenshot of the second meaning of shuq with teshuqah (in Hebrew letters) As it appears in Gesenius' lexicon. Teshuqah may simply mean "desire". If so, it is the context which supplies what kind of desire is being spoken of.[6]

TESHUQAH AND THE CONTEXT OF GENESIS 3:16

There have been several ways of understanding what "desire" means in the context of Genesis 3:16. Here are four of the more common interpretations. 1. A woman will desire a husband and marriage despite the pain that comes with having children. When God speaks to the woman in Genesis 3:16, he begins by telling her that having children will be a painful experience. It is immediately after God gives this information that he says, "your desire will be for your husband . . ." So perhaps we are meant to understand that even though childbirth and child rearing will involve pain and sorrow, a woman will still desire to be married and have a family. (In the days before contraceptives, the primary reason for marriage in practically all cultures was to raise a family.) The use of the word "yet" in the NRSV and NASB indicates that this may be the preferred interpretation of the NRSV and NASB translators: ". . . in pain you will bring forth children; Yet your desire will be for your husband . . ." (NASB, italics added) 2. A woman will desire marriage and sex despite this intimacy being marred by her husband's rule. Instead of looking at the preceding phrases, perhaps we are meant to look at the last phrase of Genesis 3:16 ("he will rule over her") to give us the context of teshuqah. If so, then the meaning is that a woman will desire to be married, and have a longing for her husband, even though the intimacy and joy of marriage will be marred by her husband's rule. The use of the word "but" in the CEB translation indicates that this may be their preferred interpretation: "You will desire your husband, but he will rule over you." (Italics added) Some have understood the woman's desire to be sexual lust, rather than simply a longing for, or a longing towards, a husband. Keil and Delitzsch include an overstatement in their commentary on Genesis 3:16 describing the woman's teshuqah as an almost manic desire: "she was punished with a desire bordering upon disease (תשוקה from שוק to run, to have a violent craving for a thing)."[7] 3. A wife's own desires are submitted to her husband. Another interpretation found in quite a few older commentaries is that a woman's own desires, or the determination of her own will,[8] will be submitted and referred to her husband, and he will grant or deny her desires as he sees fit.[9] This disturbing interpretation, and variations on it, seem to have been popular in the last several centuries.[10] 4. A wife will desire to control her husband. Foh's interpretation, adopted by some, is that a women will desire to control her husband,[11] but, despite this desire, her husband will rule her. Foh bases her interpretation on a comparison of Genesis 3:16 with Genesis 4:7 where the keywords teshuqah and mashal ("rule") also occur. However, there are some significant differences between Genesis 3:16 and 4:7. In Genesis 4:7, sin is unmistakably depicted as Cain's adversary, crouching at the door; and Cain is told that he must master sin and that this is the right thing to do. Foh believes Eve is similarly presented in Genesis 3:16 as Adam's adversary, but this is not explicit in the text.[12] Furthermore, while Cain is directly told by God to master or rule sin, Adam is nowhere told by God to master or rule Eve. In fact, God never tells men to rule women. The "rule" spoken of in Genesis 3:16 is a consequence of sin. It is not divinely commanded, as in 4:7, and it does not refer to a beneficial rule.[13] The contexts of 3:16 and 4:7 are different, even though they share two keywords.[14] Update: the meaning of "single-minded devotion" is given in this more recent article.

In Genesis 3:16 and 4:7 in the Septuagint (LXX), the Greek Old Testament, teshuqah is translated as apostrophē.[15][16] The etymology of apostrophē gives the meaning "a turning away", but it is has a broader range of meanings, some of which are conflicting. Liddell, Scott and Jones (LSJ), arguably one of the best lexicons of Ancient Greek, has several definitions for apostrophē. Most don't fit the context of Genesis 3:16 at all. For definition III, however, the LSJ says that apostrophē is used rhetorically when one turns away from all others to one person and addresses him specifically.[17] This meaning makes good sense in the contexts of Genesis 3:16 and 4:7. Since the preposition pros ("towards") also occurs in Genesis 3:16 ("your turning (apostrophē) will be towards (pros) your husband"), I think the meaning of a woman turning away from others to turn towards, or even long for, her husband may well be what is intended here.[18] Skip Moen believes that teshuqah may not mean "desire" and he looks to the early Greek, Syriac, and Coptic translations, for insight. He writes, "But there is another translation stream arising through the LXX, the Syriac Peshitta and Coptic translations. This stream views the rare Hebrew word teshuqah as "turning," not "lust." If this stream is correct, then the word in Genesis 3:16 is about Eve's mistake of "turning" her principle devotion toward Adam rather than God. Eve makes Adam her priority . . . ."[19] Walter Kaiser likewise states that teshuqah should be understood as "turning". The Hebrew word teshuqah, now almost universally translated as 'desire,' was previously rendered as 'turning.' The word appears in the Hebrew Old Testament only three times: here in Genesis 3:16, in Genesis 4:7 and in Song of Songs 7:10. Of the twelve known ancient versions (the Greek Septuagint, the Syriac Peshitta, the Samaritan Pentateuch, the Old Latin, the Sahidic, the Bohairic, the Ethiopic, the Arabic, Aquila's Greek, Symmachus's Greek, Theodotion's Greek and the Latin Vulgate), almost every one (twenty-one out of twenty-eight times) renders these three instances of teshuqah as "turning," not "desire." Likewise, the church fathers (Clement of Rome, Irenaeus, Tertullian, Origen, Epiphanius and Jerome, along with Philo, a Jew who died about A.D. 50) seem to be ignorant of any other sense for this word teshuqah than the translation of "turning." Furthermore, the Latin rendering was conversio and the Greek was apostrophē or epistrophē, words all meaning "a turning".[20] While Susan Foh, and a few others, see a power struggle implied in Genesis 3:16b, women turning towards their husbands, rather than having a desire to control them, fits better with what we see in the world at large.

CONCLUSION

There is ample evidence that, due to the prevalence of patriarchy, men have ruled their wives. God's prophetic description that "he will rule over you" has been played out in countless marriages across millennia across the globe. Over the centuries, many Christians have even assumed that Genesis 3:16 gave men permission to rule and control their wives, but there is no divine mandate here. Is there widespread evidence that women have typically desired to control their husbands, even if this desire has been thwarted by male rule? If there is, I haven't seen it. The precise meaning of teshuqah is not certain. It may mean "desire". It may mean "turning". But context, as well as the evidence from history and the present day, seems to rule out that it means "a desire to control". Whatever its meaning, the mutuality and unity between the first couple was spoiled by sin. Yet this is not the end of the story. Thankfully, Jesus came to deal with sin, and our relationships today can potentially be as mutual and harmonious as it was in Eden before the Fall (Gen. 2:21-25). Restored relationships between men and women is part of the good news of Jesus.

Endnotes

1] Susan T. Foh, "What is the Woman's Desire?", The Westminster Theological Journal 37 (1974/75), 376-83. This paper can be read online.

[2] Song of Solomon (Song of Songs, or Canticles) 7:11 in the Septuagint is equivalent to 7:10 in English and Hebrew Bibles.

[3] Francis Brown, "תְּשׁוּקָה", The Brown-Driver-Briggs Hebrew and English Lexicon. (Peabody, MA: Hendrickson, 2007), 1003.

[4] Ibid., 1003. Unlike what some online resources suggest, BDB does not connect teshuqah with Strong's words 7783, 7784 or 7785. These are unrelated words spelt שׁוּק—shuq and שׁוֹק—shoq. The Strong's number for teshuqah is 8669. There

is no Strong's number for the shuq which is the primitive and obsolete stem of teshuqah. Moreover, there is no clear consensus among lexicographers as to what the meanings of this particular stem were. [5] Friedrich Wilhelm Gesenius, "שׁוּק", Gesenius' Hebrew-Chaldee Lexicon to the Old Testament Scriptures, English translation by Samuel Prideaux Tregelles (London: Samuel Bagster and Sons) (Source)

[6] David T. Lang has found eleven occurrences of teshuqah in Qumran sectarian manuscripts, most of which are translated as "longing" or "desire." He writes, "Interestingly, in most of these cases the object of desire was something negative or in some way related to destruction. The desire spoken of was not clearly a 'desire for control,' but it certainly seemed to connote some kind of negative longing or obsession." (Source) Since the members of the Qumran community were ascetics, and desire was antithetical to a strictly disciplined lifestyle, it is not surprising that they viewed desire and longing negatively.

[7] C.F. Keil and F. Delitzsch, "The Pentateuch", Biblical Commentary: The Old Testament, Vol. 1, English translation by James Martin (Edinburgh: T. & T, Clark, 1885), 108. (Sources 1 and 2)

[8] Albert Barnes, Notes on the Old Testament (London, Blackie & Son, 1884) (Source)

[9] Joseph Benson, Commentary of the Old and New Testament (New York: T. Carlton & J. Porter, 1867), (Source).

[10] For example: "'Thy desire shall be unto thy husband,' is of the same force as if he had said that she should not be free and at her own command, but subject to the authority of her husband and dependent upon his will; or as if he had said, 'Thou shalt desire nothing but what thy husband wishes.'" John Calvin, Commentary on Genesis. (Source) A few older commentaries on Genesis 3:16, here.

[11] In his commentary on Genesis 3:16 in the ESV Study Bible, T. Desmond Alexander agrees with Foh's interpretation and writes that this verse "indicates that there will be an ongoing struggle between the woman and the man for leadership in the marriage relationship. . . . Eve will have the sinful 'desire' to

oppose Adam and assert leadership over him." ESV Study Bible (Wheaton, IL: Crossway, 2008), 56.

[12] The two obvious adversaries in Genesis 3 are the cursed serpent, who will be an enemy especially of the woman and her seed (Gen. 3:15), and the cursed ground (adamah), which will produce thorns and thistles and make life especially hard for Adam (Gen. 3:17-19).

[13] The form of mashal used in Genesis 3:16 is identical to that in Isaiah 19:4, and similar to that in Proverbs 17:2.

[14] For more on the contexts of Genesis 3:16 and 4:7 see Irvin A. Busenitz's paper, "Woman's Desire for Man: Genesis 3:16 Reconsidered", Grace Theological Journal 7.2 (1986), 203-12, esp. 206-210. This paper can be read online here.

[15] The Greek word which translates teshuqah in Song of Solomon 7 is epistrophē which has a somewhat different range of meanings to apostrophē.

[16] Interestingly, the Hebrew word teshuvah (which looks similar to teshuqah) means a "turning" or "return", etc. This word is derived from the root שׁוּב—shuv. Shuv and teshuvah are neither rare nor obscure words. (More on shuv here.) Is teshuqah really meant to be the word teshuvah?

 [17] Henry George Liddell and Robert Scott, "apostrophē", A Greek-English Lexicon, Ninth Edition, revised by Sir Henry Stuart Jones, with the assistance of Roderick McKenzie (Oxford, UK: Clarendon, 1996), 220.

[18] Pros corresponds with the Hebrew preposition el- אֶל which occurs in the Hebrew text of Genesis 3:16. BDB (page 39) gives the general definition of el as a "preposition denoting motion to or direction towards." The ESV translates it as "for" in Genesis 3:16, but gives an alternate meaning in a footnote of "against". El is occasionally used in a hostile sense; nevertheless it typically means "towards". Perhaps the debate over the meaning of Genesis 3:16 needs to focus more on this preposition than on the meanings of teshuqah and apostrophē. Update: The latest version (August 2016) of the ESV translates Genesis 3:16a as: "Your desire shall be contrary

to your husband . . ." This seems like a paraphrase or interpretation, rather than a literal translation.

[19] You can read more of Skip Moen's interpretation here. (I have changed his use of the more Hebraic "Havah" to the more recognisable "Eve" in the quote.)

[20] Walter Kaiser et al, "3:16 How was the Woman Punished?", Hard Sayings of the Bible (Downers Grove, IL: InterVarsity Press, 1996), 96.[4]

4

SUBMISSION:THE REAL TRUTH

"Do you need me or do you need someone? There is a difference."

~Rupi Kaur~

As we begin this chapter on submission, I am so very careful as to how I approach this because I know that this is a very sensitive subject, hence the title of this chapter. When talking about submission in the church, it is like saying a cuss word. This one subject is like releasing expletives into the air because it is a very touchy issue which remains a hot-button issue among the religious community. I am addressing the church primarily due to the contentions in our church culture today in relation to gender roles, family life, and other related problems that flow over into business and the business sector.

It is a harsh reality that submission is a one-way street for women-in the minds and the hearts of many people in our society. The proof is, it has permeated our society in such a way that even though it may be unspoken, it manifests in the attitudes of many men in authority; Not only in Christian circles is this an issue, but in business circles and in the business world and its environments. The pervasive ideology is still that of women being quiet, perfecting her abilities as nurturers, and remaining submitted to either her husband, boss or male pastor. In order for this subject matter to be dealt with objectively within the pages of this book, I'm going to have to dissect a few verses of Scripture, and break down the proper translation of some common Greek words that are going to help us understand this doctrine and its origins. It is so very important as we approach this erroneous philosophy, we must apply systematic research that is credible which will ensure that our ending conclusions are indeed accurate and inerrant.

For the sake of foundation, let's begin first with the understanding that for some of us who have grown up in the church, and it doesn't matter whether that church   was a Lutheran church, Catholic, Presbyterian, Pentecostal, Apostolic or any other denominational church; For many, the teachings about women and submission originate with the things they have been taught in church and also within the home. These thoughts about submission and women being quiet are highly pervasive throughout a great many denominations- including some that have not been mentioned. One of the things that we have to look at as well is the fact that Jesus brought forth an egalitarian model for all relationships in that there was no such thing as someone else ruling over the other in the sense of dominating them and controlling them. We use the term egalitarian, even though it is not a word that's found in scripture- however, it is a philosophy and a way of thinking, that best describes the way that Jesus dealt with women.

When we look back in the scripture and we see how that the spirit of the Lord fell, He was not only poured out on men. God included women when He released His Spirit. So this first and foremost reinforces the idea that this ideology is correct. There is no hierarchy between men and women. There is no one gender or sex that is above or beneath the other. The egalitarian philosophy is correct. The thought that man has to be the "go- between" God and woman is utterly ridiculous. *"There is only one mediator between God and man (woman), the man Jesus Christ."(*1 Tim.2:5) And we have very many incidences such as Agabus, who was a prophet, who had daughters who prophesied and the spirit of God rested on them and they prophesied themselves. (Acts21:8-10) So we see that the Spirit of the Lord was without predjudice in His manifestation to both men and women.

We then come to the conclusion or draw the inference that whatever we're going to see after Jesus written in the Book of Acts or in the Epistlesit is gong to be the same model, ideology and doctrine as is portrayed by Christ in the Gospels. We must take into account the historicity of the texts. If we do not look at the pervasive culture of the time, we're going to miss the message that is being conveyed and intended for those that the writers were addressing. As a theologian, one must not discount those historical and cultural issues that are contained in the rich tapestry within the chapters.

Making close observations of these things, we must make sure that we have the correct meaning and understanding. One of the points that I would like for us to bring attention to is going to come from the Scripture in First Corinthians 11:2-16(ESV)

> "Now, I commend you because you remember me and everything and maintain the traditions even as I deliver them to you, but I want you to understand that the head of every man is Christ. The head of the wife, the head of a wife is her husband. The head of Christ is God. Every man who prays or prophesies with his head covered dishonors his head, but every wife who prays or prophesies with her head uncovered dishonors her head, since it is the same as if her head was shaven. For if a wife will not have her head covered, then she should cut her hair short. But since it is disgraceful for a wife to cut off our hair or shave her head, let her head be covered. For a man ought not to cover his head since he is the image and glory of God, but woman is the glory of Man. For man was not made from woman, but woman from man, neither was man created for woman, but woman for man. That is why a wife ought to have a symbol of authority on her head, because of the angels. Nevertheless, in the Lord, woman is not independent of man, nor man or woman, for woman was made from man, so man is now born of a woman. And all things are from God. Judge, for yourselves, is it proper for a wife to pray to God with her head uncovered? Does not nature itself teach you that if a man wears long hair, it is a disgrace for him. But if a woman has long hair is her glory, for her hair is given to her for a covering. If anyone is inclined to be contentious, we have no such practice nor do the churches of God."

Looking at these verses and then also surveying the book of Ephesians will bring clarity and understanding of Paul's message being conveyed to the Corinthian church as well as the true emphasis of his message. Ephesians chapter 5 verses 21 through 23 (ESV) and it says,

> "Submitting to one another out of reverence for Christ. Wives, submit to your own husbands as to the Lord, for the husband is the head of the wife even as Christ ahead of the church, his body and is himself, its savior. Now, as the church submits to Christ, so also wives should submit in everything to their husbands. Husbands, love your wives as Christ loved the church and gave himself up for her that he might sanctify her. Having cleansed her by the washing of the water with the word so that he might present the church to himself in splendor without spot or wrinkle or any such thing that she might be holy and without blemish. In the same way, husbands should love their wives as their own bodies. He who loves his wife, loves himself for no one ever hated his own flesh, but nourishes and cherishes it just as Christ does the church, because we are members of his body. Therefore, a man shall leave his father and mother and hold fast to his wife. And the two shall become one flesh. This mystery is profound, and I'm saying that it refers to Christ and the church. However, let each one of you love his wife as himself and let the wife see that she respects her husband."

There you have it, right? It's as plain as the words on the page we are reading. Or is it? As we look at this, I would like to begin dealing with one of the Greek words used in this verse. When we look at the word "head" as is a mentioned here in Ephesians chapter five. Now this word "head", is used in several verses of scripture. It is used in First Corinthians chapter 11, verses two through 16 as we have already read, it is also mentioned in Ephesians Chapter Four Verses 15 and 23. It is also mentioned in Ephesians within verses 21 through 23; And also Colossians 1:18; 2:10,18 so looking at this, this word is a very common word that is used in the scripture, but I want to break down the Greek word used in these verses for "head."

The Greek word used in the verses above for "head" is Kephale.

"The meaning of Kephale. The central New Testament doctrine allegedly mandating subordination of women is the Pauline doctrine of "Headship". The doctrine springs from the Greek word Kephale which has been translated by the English word "head." Because today kephale does not mean "head" in the modern sense of "authority over" or "leadership," we easily misinterpret kephale passages making them say something Paul never intended." and this work can follow, does not mean head in the sense of 'authority over' or 'leadership.' Nevertheless, hierarchs continue to maintain that kephale means 'head' in the sense of 'authority over.' In terms of gender, they maintain a patriarchal order based on the premise that men are destined by God to rule as authoritative leaders over women. In terms of church government, they hold to the chain-of-command authority structure which they describe as 'divine order,' usually involving apostolic succession in an institutional framework." [1]

"A study by Alvera and the late Berkeley Mickelsen is an example of such research. They reported their finding in "The 'Head' of the Epistles" (Christianity Today, Feb. 20, 1981). They provide strong evidence that, in biblical Greek, kephale cannot mean "superior to" or "one having authority." They garner support for their position from Liddell, Scott, Jones and McKenzie (A Greek-English Lexicon, 9th ed., Clarendon Press, 1940) which renders the meaning as "source" with no implication of hierarchy or authority. Furthermore, they point out that the Greek scholar, Walter Bauer, does not provide support for his personal, hierarchical interpretation of Paul's use of kephale (A Greek-English Lexicon of the New Testament and Early Christian Literature, Wm. Arndt and F. W. Gingrich, eds., U. of Chicago Press, 1957/1979).

Perhaps the Mickelsen's most valuable contribution to the discussion is their study of kephale in the Septuagint. This scholarly couple studied how the Hebrew/Greek scholars who translated the Hebrew Scriptures (i.e. Old Testament) dealt with the Hebrew word ro'sh, the Hebrew word meaning 'head'. They discovered that ro'sh occurs 180 times in the

Hebrew text, but these learned translators used kephale to translate ro'sh only six times. Where the Hebrew text conveyed the meaning 'ruler', 'commander' 'leader,' however, they used the Greek word archon. The translators, in fact, avoided the use of kephale when the passage included the idea of 'authority over' because they understood that kephale did not commonly carry this meaning. The Apostle Paul, also an astute scholar, was also aware of this. If he had wanted to convey the sense of 'one having authority over or leadership of,' he would have used archon or other authority-laden words rather than kephale.

The Mickelsen's discovered that the Septuagint translators used fourteen different Greek words to convey the various meanings of the Hebrew word ro'sh (head). These include the following:

1. archon (ruler,commander, leader) 109 times
2. archegos (captain, leader, chief, prince) 10 times
3. arche (authority, magistrate, officer) 9 times
4. hegeomai (to be a leader, rule, have dominion) 9 times
5. protos (first or foremost) 6 times
6. patriarches (father or chief of a race, patriarch) 3 times
7. chiliarches (commander) 3 times
8. achipules (chief of a tribe) 2 times
9. achipatriotes (head of a family) 1 time
10. archo (verb; ruler, be ruler of) 1 time
11. megas, magale, mega (great, mighty, very important) 1 time
12. proegeomai (take the lead, go first, lead the way) 1 time
13. prototokos (firstborn or first in rank) 1 time
14. kephale (where head can mean top or crown) 8 times
    kephale (in head-tail metaphor) 4 times

    kephale (manuscripts have variant readings 6 times

    ro'sh (not translated) 6 times [2]

Did you get it? After you study this word, you realise and gain an understanding of what Paul is teaching the church. In laymen's terms, the word "head" in Ephesians chapter 5 when properly translated kephale means means source of life. And it's talking about creation. It is clear that this word has been misinterpreted and erroneously transliterated to take on a meaning that is clearly incorrect. There is no question that this word is not speaking of authority or leadership. It is talking about man being a source of life. So, when we use this word or when we look at this word in the verses that I have mentioned, you must understand that the reference is toward a woman who came out of man, which was Adam in creation. Paul is saying that the man was the source of the woman in creation and now she has become the source of man in procreation - meaning the coming together of a man and a woman to create a baby! And so that's what we see in First Corinthians chapter 11. When you read the Greek lexicon, you will see that this word is rendered as source and there's no other implication with these words whatsoever about any type of hierarchy, any form of authority or any form of one being over the other in a dominant manner.

I would like to also use as a reference the fact that the New Testament is translated from the Greek. That being an established fact, we know that it was translated from the Septuagint. When you look in the Septuagint when it's using the word for authority in the verse mentioned, it does not use the word kephale. It uses the Word archon so we must make sure that we understand when Paul is making the statement, he's talking about creation when he's talking about man being the head of the wife and Christ being the head of man. Christ is the source of man, man is the source for women and this is creative or a creational explanation and that is all that it is. It is not authoritative or hierarchical at all. We must understand that what kephale or head is making reference to.

Another idea that is very popular today in some of the churches complementarianism. It simply is it means that men and women perfect or supplement bring each other into perfection in the different roles that they carry and their responsibilities. It's not a hierarchical mindset. However, this thinking still says that there are specific roles for men and specific roles for women, and although they are not oppressive in nature in their belief system, complementarianism is still not the correct view.

Neither is the traditionalist view, which means wives should be quiet, women should be silent in the church, you're to marry, have children and guide the house. You know, the traditional things that we have always been taught. We must pay special attention to what Paul said in Ephesians when was addressing the Ephesians Believers. Before he says for wives to submit themselves to their husbands, he says first, that we should submit ourselves to one another in love; Which means that in marriage, there is a mutually submitted relationship between a man and a woman. When we're using the word kephale, it is most absolutely conveying the same idea of equality that is expressed throughout the New Testament and the message that Jesus brought forth.

Now let's talk about marriage in the Greco-Roman world. The reason that we need to discuss this is because there's no way for us to really ascertain a proper understanding of the lifestyle change that Paul was conveying to the readers of his letter, unless we grasp the prevailing cultural issues with which the Church existed within. We must first understand the situations that were taking place during that time. I would like to use movies as an example to lay the groundwork. First and foremost, in every movie that you see, especially all of the old Roman movies show that there were times during that era that they had orgies and illicit behavior sexually and moraly. One of the ideas that is usually hidden from some of the old Roman movies is the idea that in that particular society, homosexuality was a superior relationship.

When juxtaposed to heterosexual relationship, homosexuality was the preferred lifestyle of that time, society and culture. And the reason that was, is because during that time, women were considered to be unequal. Women were considered evil, unclean and inferior. Therefore, since that was the thought of the day, it was preferred that men would have relationships with men. So when we go back and we see Paul dealing with First Corinthians chapter 11 and he's making a plea to the people, he's dealing with the mindset of these people who understood that homosexuality was looked at as a higher relationship than that between a man and a woman. He understood that women were looked upon as property, and also as unclean, evil, inferior, and unequal. Yes, I repeatd this twice because this mindset was pervasive within the Roman culture. Part of his goal in the message that he was conveying, was reinforcing the idea of marriage between a man and a woman versus the homosexual lifestyle and relationship that was prevalent during that time. For the Apostle Paul to use this word kephale, it is so very essential to understand the mindset of the one who was teaching. So, for him to say kephale, when he is talking about the man being the head and Christ being the head, - he's talking about the source of woman, not archon. Remember there are two different words. Archon and kephale that are used when the New Testament is talking about the "head." So, for the sake of repetition, this word kephale is source. And archon is ruler.

Paul was taking a stand against the ungodly belief system of his day. He was standing up for the woman in all actuality and declaring that woman was not a lesser individual than man in his explanation. This was understood by those who were receiving his message. In his explanation, he was essentially affirming the idea that woman was indeed fit as a partner in life. That woman was indeed fit to be the companion of man because now he's reinforcing the idea that woman is now kephale with man in creation or procreation as he states.

When we go back and we look at First Corinthians chapter 11 and you look at verse 12, you see this affirmation about the equality of the man and a woman together, when he speaks and says, "neither is the woman independent of the man or the man or the woman in the Lord, for just as the woman is from man. So man is from the woman in all things are of God." Paul's powerful message is leveling the playing field and he's tearing down those pagan mindsets, establishing something that was never there for the people in this Greco-Roman era and in this world. Their mindset was that homosexuality was a higher form of relationship and that heterosexual relationships were not to be sought after because no one wanted a woman who was considered unclean, evil, inferior, and unequal. When you look at Ephesians chapter five, now we have to bring everything into the perspective that I was speaking of before. We must apply the text's historicity, and the cultural perspective of what was taking place during this time. There's no way to really comprehend unless you observe the history of the Greco-Roman world and understand why Paul was speaking so specifically.

On the one hand, he's dealing with a mindset of people who were bound by paganism and believed that homosexual relationships where above heterosexuality and that male-to-male companionship was the ideal relationship. Culturally, heterosexual relationships were not to be sought after. Since women were unclean, evil, inferior and unequal. The pervasive thought was that a man felt that only another man could truly be an equal partner. Paul was bringing understanding to a group of people who were formerly pagans. The goal of his message was to help them grasp that elevating the woman within the culture and also within relationships was important to God and to their divine assignment in the earth. If he were talking to the Jews who already understood what God's intention was in creation, there would've been no need for him to express the mind of God regarding manhood, womanhood, or marital relationship roles. Jews already understood creation. They had been taught these things from childhood; but because he was dealing with former- pagan converts who were unlearned in the Scriptures, It was necessary for him to establish order from creation, as he laid doctrinal foundations for their new Faith. Since he was dealing with a people who had a different mindset about what man and woman's purpose was, he had to establish the reality of what they were actually created to do, which brings us back to reading Ephesians chapter five.

The background that I have provided helps to establish why he is speaking with such specificity about the marriage and submission. This must be addressed one layer at a time. When we look at what marriage was like in this Roman empire or the Greco- Roman world, it is not without notice as we study history, that there were many different forms of marriage. One of the forms of marriage during that time was Sine Manu. In this type of marriage, the wife was legally and ritually, a member of her father's family. She remained a part of her father's family for the duration of her marital relationship. Paul had to give an explanation concerning a husband and how he would leave his mother and father and cleave to his wife. He then expresses in scripture why it is important for husband and wife to embrace this new relational dynamic being expressed in his teachings.

Standing under this control would be the woman, who remained under the control/authority of her father's power or what they call "protestos." She, the wife, though married, remained under her father's protestos/power. This is how the marriages were governed, so he became like a magistrate in the law for his daughter or daughter in law. It would be that she would either stay under the power of her father, a father-in-law or the oldest patriarch in her husband's family. and so they had what they called "Patria Potestas" which is the father's power. The wife would live under the power of the father. This is very important because during this period in history, the wife in this particular type of marriage, had to remain connected and attached to her birth patriarch-the oldest father in the family. She had to stay connected to them-so she was not really under her husband's guidance, control or authority at all according to Roman Marital Law!. I repeat, She was **not** under her husband's authority. She was not really officially a part of his house. She was still a part of her father's house though she was married to her husband! So when Paul is writing in this chapter in Ephesians 5, that we are discussing, he's talking to these Believers who are new converts- that were formally pagans that come out of this lifestyle, who understand that their wives are not submitted to them because they are submitted to "Patria Potestas," their father's power.

 His discourse in this letter to the Ephesians is really birthing and unveiling to them a new revelation about what marriage as Believers is supposed to look like on the other side of the Cross. Again, bringing everything to a head, it is to be understood that nowhere in these verses is there anything about subordination of women to men. It needs to be understood that this is Paul conveying to the people what it is that is in the very heart of God for his people as it pertains to Christian marriage. Paul's teaching also conveys with it the idea that husbands should be caring emotionally, (Eph. 5:25) and that they should be intimate sexually (Eph. 5:28). This is a very important point for many reasons, one of which is that he is raising the level of thought concerning women against the prevailing cultural norms and he's shattering

Mindsets, concepts and belief systems that are pervasive in their society. In order for him to do that, he must introduce something new to them by explaining the scripture and then affirming what God has created while revealing what God intended for humanity within our relationships as Born-Again Believers. Formerly, we didn't know God's ways. We didn't understand how God created us to function. We didn't understand what His will is or was for us. All we knew where our family traditions, the things we learned out there in a life of sin. But when we were born again, began to attend church and learn the word of God, as we learned, we understood that our old way of doing things was not the right way. We understood that what we thought was right, we came to learn that it was incorrect.

Why? Because a new concept, a new revelation was introduced to us through the word of God and through those who taught us the word of God. They helped us to understand that what we once believed, no matter what our society taught us, once we came in to Christ, we had to let go of those mindsets. Likewise, this is what Paul is doing. Paul is introducing to these new Believers what God intends for them. What His will is for them. What his mindset is for them and what He ordained for them before the foundation of the world- that heterosexual marriage is right. And not just that heterosexual marriage is right, but that grasping the meaning of kephale- that man and woman together are the source of life. Paul defined and clarified the purpose of man and woman coming together. Paul reveal how that the husband and the wife should dwell together in love being able to care for each other, being able to love one another and not rule over the other. Though these things were pervasive in society at that time, Paul had to do deep teaching in order to uproot all of those false doctrines, those false pagan doctrines - to impart the truth of the word of God.

There is no way we could get into our main subject matter without dealing with kephale. We're going to deal with submission and I'm going to break down this word submission because it is so very important that what is the what is spoken of in the title of this book is addressed. It is a matter of urgency that we understand that society's and the church's double standards must be addressed and torn down. We must axe every myth and the lies concerning submission and silence of women in order that every woman would be able to stand in her proper places as women endowed by God without any shred of doubt. Women have been given the power of the Spirit of God to be able to fulfill every assignment they've been given. Whether that means becoming wives, sisters or mothers, pastors and prophets, evangelists, teachers or judges, and ceo's of fortune 500 companies. Whatever it is, we must shatter these myths so that we can stand in the truth. The only way that we can stand in the truth is that we must first learn the truth, believe it, live it and teach others!

Let's delve into this a little further and look at Colossians chapter one, verse 18. Going through a few verses here will enable us to get a better understanding and be able to address this word kephale in some of the other verses. Look at Colossians Chapter One and read the 18th verse, verse 18 is very plain. it says,

"And he is the head of the body, the church. He is the beginning, he firstborn from the dead. That in everything he might be preeminent." And this word is the Greek word head, kephale- which means the head of the corner, the chief cornerstone, the head. It is not talking about hierarchy. He's talking about his position. He's talking about the fact that He Himself, because again, kephali has been rendered in the Greek lexicon as source. So He, Christ is the source. So let's read that verse again and see what it says. And it says in verse 18, "He is the source of the body, the church. He is the beginning, the firstborn from the dead, and that in everything, He might be preeminent." It is obviously restated that this means that he is the source.

Let me just take a quick break and deal with the word "source" a little further and give a simple definition of what source is. Webster's dictionary gives a very good definition of the word "source" and it says the following: a point of origin or procurement, beginning. It is one that initiates. The author and prototype.[3] This makes perfect sense when you look at how kephale is translated in Colossians 1:18, understanding that Christ is the source of the body or He is the author of the body; the one who supplies what is needed for the body, He's the prototype for the body. He is the point of origin for the body. Breaking the word down in this manner helps us to understand the proper meaning and appropriate usage of the word "head," (kephale), which is chief cornerstone, or the simple form of the word is "source." So the purpose of what has been shared in First Corinthians and in Colossians is to bring clarity to the overall message that is being conveyed in those chapters. This helps to grasp a better understanding that the translations of the word "head" are not defined with any notion that means anything concerning authority. It is simply talking about being the "source." If we are going to teach the Scripture, we must make sure that we understand with accuracy the message the Scripture is conveying. The Scriptures mentioned are NOT expressing that man is the (archon) "ruler over" a woman, but that he is the (kephale) source of woman; because in creation, woman came out of man and now in procreation, man comes out of woman. For interpretation sake, it is very important that we do not ascribe to the scripture something that is not expressed therein. We must understand when reading and interpreting the Scripture, its context; and that text out of context, is no text at all. In essence, we butcher the text and its intended meaning when we add or remove the original appellations assigned to it, along with the environment in which it was spoken and its context to the original audience. Study of any subject must include adequate research. Thorough Research of scripture should include its pre-text, post-text and context. It is also paramount to include cultural information as well as historicity. All of the aforementioned, must be done before one establishes their interpretation as doctrinally sound.

Going back to Ephesians chapter 5, take a look at verse 18 through 22. It says, "wives, submit to your own husbands as to the Lord, for the husband is the head of the wife." We will not restate what has already been established in the previous paragraphs. Instead, let's look at the word submit. This word in context in verse 22, is not what we think it is. Why must we deal with submission? Having already interpreted "authority," we understand that the words that we have been looking at as authority over women is actually not expressing authority over women. Therefore, if what has been previously understood has been erroneously established, the entire context of each word must be revisited along with the accurate interpretation and meaning.

So now that we've broken that down, we must address the submission or the subjugation of women to men in society, business, church and in the home. This topic must be unearthed further if we are to get to the truth of the matter and establish with accuracy the orthodoxy of biblical gender roles. If we're going to walk in freedom as Believers, and biblical inerrancy as theologians, we must unmask the error, myths and lies that have been taught for generations. When Paul says, "wives, submit to your own husbands;" the word "submit" in English is used and translated hupotasso.

"Hupotasso can mean 'to show responsible behavior towards others.'

Hupotasso can mean 'to be brought into a sphere of influence.'

Hupotasso can mean 'to add or unite one person or thing with another.'

Paul's Use of the Household Code.

1. Paul found it necessary to advise his converts about family relationships (Eph 5), beginning with something they understood (Household Code) and leading them to something different from what they had known, that is, Christian Marriage.
2. In Ephesians 5:18-33 Paul is describing Christian marriage, asking husband and wife to be committed to one another only (v.31) in an atmosphere of mutual identification and unity (v.21).
a. He asks a married woman to identify with(hupotasso) and be committed to her husband rather than to her birth family.
b. He asks children and slaves to obey (hupakouo)
c. He asks a husband to love (agape) his wife (a new idea) and to submit (hupotasso) to his wife (v.21).
3. Unilateral obedience and subjugation of the wife to the husband is not a biblical doctrine.
4. The issues here are identity and unity (husband and wife as a cohesive unit of equal partners), sameness of substance and equality in value.
5. Accurately interpreted, the passage does not promote authoritative male dominance and female subjugation.[4]

Family life in the Greco-Roman world of the New Testament era was from our point of view, dysfunctional. Paul therefore found it necessary to advise his converts about family relationships (Eph. 5).

This idea of mutual identification and unity occurs in various other passages. Consider, for example, 1 Corinthians 7:3-4;

Galatians 5:13; Philippians 2:3; 1 Peter 3:7. Indeed, the thrust of New Testament relationships and of Christian marriage revolves around mutuality and interdependence, not patriarchy and authority over/subordination to others. Again, in understanding Paul's words in Ephesians 5 regarding hupotasso, it is a critical to remember the low status of women and the dysfunctional nature of marriage in the Greco-Roman world. These are the issues underlying Paul's address. He would have women, not despised, used and abused, but cherished and valued as equal with men. The issues here are identity and unity (husband and wife as a cohesive unit of equal partners), sameness of substance, and equality in value. Accurately interpreted, the passage does not promote authoritative male dominance and female subjugation.[5]

The above statements and explained interpretations of the Greek words used in the passages of Scripture most commonly referenced to subjugate women, makes it quite clear- in plain English, the majority of the Church-world as we know it, have been hoodwinked and bamboozled into believing something that is utterly false doctrinally, and erroneous historically. The only way to right these fallacies, is to question what has been accepted as orthodoxy and teach the truth!

This chapter, I am sure, will cause quite a stir among those who, even after reading and source-checking, will find a way to discredit the proves presented, and remain stuck in an erroneous paradigm of thinking and teaching- all because of traditions and affinities to organisations.

May these words and explanations break men and women out of their cages of false doctrine and bring them into the liberty that the Truth of the Gospel of Jesus Christ is meant to give all mankind.

5

WHAT DID JESUS DO?

We have taken a good, hard look at several perspectives thus far. I want to begin here by evaluating the way that Jesus dealt with women. I know it's easy for us to say that Jesus lifted women, but I want us to look at the prevailing mindset that was pervasive in the culture as Jesus encountered them. We're going to read through some verses that show us that men did not think it was appropriate for Jesus to engage in conversation with women. Why? Because women were supposed to be subordinated, submitted, and silent. As we explore this cultural and religious mindset towards women, we will see women were thought of as property; Not only were they classified as property, but it was also believed that women were unequal, inferior, evil and that they were unclean. I would encourage every person that can, to pick up a copy of "Veiled and Silenced: How Culture Shapes Sexist Theology, by Alvin John Schmidt. I believe that some of the prevailing theological thoughts that we deal with today, you will see that they were also pervasive in earlier societies- as documented in the book mentioned above and during the period Jesus walked the earth.

In his book, Schmidt deals with women living with the labels as evil, inferior, unclean and as unequal to men. He also discusses how culture as a whole has shaped our theology and how these labels came to be applied to women through the years. He doesn't stop there. He tackles the ongoing fight for the equality of women with honesty, historical proof and integrity. Here are a few brief snippets of his thoughts and notes on the historical context of this struggle through the ages.

That women should be silent was still a vociferous argument in the latter part of the nineteenth century when male chauvinists fought bitterly to keep women from exercising their right at the ballot box. In the United States the advocates of woman's silence finally lost their battle when the Nineteenth Amendment was ratified and became part of the American Constitution in 1920.

To many clergy in these churches, (ultraconservative or fundamentalist) it is a matter of "Thus saith the Lord." They are particularly quick to cite two New Testament references: "The woman should keep silent in the churches. For they are not permitted to speak." (1 Cor. 14:34). "I permit not a woman to teach or to have authority over men; she is to keep silent" (1 Tim 2:12).

The silencing of women is not something that is confined to sexist theology, however. Greco-Roman culture, before the Rabbis and Church Fathers brought up the subject, had deeply entrenched rules that very effectively silenced women for centuries.[1]

Greek Culture: Greek Culture is replete with references to keeping women silent. Sophocles (495-406 B.C.) said: "O woman, silence is an adornment to women" (Ajax 293). Homer portrays Telemachus rebuking his mother, Penelope, for speaking. Dogmatically, he tells her that "speech shall be for men" (The Odyssey 1,359).[2]

Roman Culture: Denying women the right to speak publicly was part of the Roman cultural syndrome. For instance, Roman fathers gave their daughters in marriage at the early age of twelve years. Once she was married, she came under the Roman institution of Cum Manus, which placed her under her husband's authority, preventing her from seriously questioning or repudiating her husband in any way. He, however, had the right to repudiate her in whatever way he wished.[3] A (Roman) woman, was never sui iuris and not a person in the legal sense.[4]

Hebrew Culture: The Hebrew Rabbis placed the prohibition of woman's speaking in the context of religion. To the Rabbis, a woman's public speech was an act that offended God. Josephus, a first-century Pharisee, apparently reflected the Hebrew religious opinion when he said that women were not to speak because the Law of Moses enjoined it (Antiquities 4.8.15).The Oral Law of the Rabbis (from about 400 B.C. to

A.D. 400), now essentially the Talmud and Mishnah, even warned against heeding a wife's private advice in the home. Said Rabbi Rab: "He who follows his wife's counsel will descend into Gehenna" (Kiddushin 59:2). In the context of the Synagogue, the Rabbis decreed: "Out of respect of the congregation, the woman should not read in the Law (Torah)" (Megillah 23a).[5]

The Postapostolic Church: The Church Fathers and their long train of successors did their utmost to keep women from teaching, preaching, and …singing in the church. In doing so unwittingly-and contrary to Christ and the Apostles-wove the ancient pagan cultural views of women into theology, which was (and still is in many quarters of the Church) heralded as the plan and will of God.

The Greco-Roman philosophers and poets simply said women were to be silent in the presence of men. They rarely, if ever, gave any reason. They didn't have to give any. It was a cultural norm, a mos, a way of life. The Church Fathers and later theologians, however, went one step farther. By arguing that women had to be silent among men because that was God's will, they not only blinded themselves from seeing centuries of sexist discrimination, but they also gave to the ancient Pagan cultural beliefs and practices a theological legitimation that they never had among the Greeks and Romans. Keeping women silent, especially in Churches, was now a matter of "Thus saith the Lord." It never occurred to the theologians that God might have been shocked to or even angered to be credited with something that was not issued from he heavenly mansion. The powerful force of ancient culture did not permit that kind of introspection.[6]

Enforced Silence Outside of Church-Worship Contexts:

Silencing women in the Western world was not just confined to worship or ecclesiastical settings. Women were not permitted to speak formally in secular gatherings when men were present. It is only since the early 1920s, after the ratification of the Nineteenth Amendment to the Constitution, that the Clergy have been saying the silence of women applies only to formal worship. Prior to the 1920s 1 Cor. 14 and 1 Tim 2 were commonly applied to prohibiting women from engaging in any type of formal, public speaking.[7]

The Anti-Suffrage Movement: Having in mind those states that already had given women the right to vote before the Nineteenth Amendment was ratified, Louis Sieck blamed them for causing women to become "masculinized in their dress and habits of speech." [8] Joseph V. McKee, writing in the journal Catholic World, maintained that woman suffrage would lead to easy divorce laws.[9] And some Catholic Bishops proclaimed the vote would be equivalent to having her become a "fallen woman." [10]

Arguments Since the Enactment of the Nineteenth Amendment: The above historical illustrations clearly indicate that countless Clergy, for centuries, unknowingly have been espousing ancient, agrarian cultural views of woman's role as "Thus saith the Lord." They are unaware that the public silencing of women was practiced by the Greeks, Romans, Hebrews and others. There is nothing godly or Christian about silencing women. The practice is virtually as old as paganism itself. If the advocates of women's silence were to examine the origins of this old, discriminatory position, many would probably see their error and help promote the of cause of women's rights.[11]

Now let's look back at Jesus. Christ conveys God's approval and affirmation of the female gender through His teachings, His approach, His dealings with and lifting of women and showing their worth by forgiving them of sins, as well as the fact that He has conversation with and gave commands to women. It is clear by the aforementioned that Jesus treated women equally to men. Jesus affirms the female's equality in substance, value, and by extending to woman, the privileges that should only be entitled to men at that time. He goes further by giving to women who followed Him, responsibilities that formerly they wouldn't have ever had. By Jesus' actions, the door is open to see women function in an entirely new and different dimension. This freed the woman to fulfill and walk in her God-ordained calling and authority.

 As we look at the scripture, we will see that Jesus dealt with women who were on different spectrums of life. The married woman and those who were single, both likewise had encounters with the Savior. Let us not forget the women who were in adulterous affairs, in various statuses of life-with illnesses and demonic possession, they too were among those who Christ either addressed, rescued or healed in the presence of others. These were not just benign meetings. The many contacts Jesus had with these women happened with the express design to create a new construct for the way woman would be handled, approached and treated in society.

By Christ handling women in the manner spoken of above, this shattered cultural and religious perspectives. Just as Jesus shattered those perspectives, this chapter will highlight what has been written in the scripture, so that whatever incorrect perspectives we may have, even deep-seated beliefs that have been ingrained in us that we may not even realize are there- those are the constructs that must be challenged. We have received mental programming from culture, we've developed mindsets that have been passed down from within our familial relationships… those are the positions that have influenced us and assisted in continuing the social and cultural bondage of the female gender. This has been perpetuated through the images that we have seen on television, in newspapers, and even what we have read in books about women. The portrayal is almost always as inferior, evil, unclean, and unequal. That will be addressed to a greater degree in a later chapter. We must shatter former patterns of thinking and bring a proper point of view to who woman has truly been created to be.

What does God really say about women and how women should live and function in this present culture? As we approach this subject, one of the pervasive ideologies that must be addressed is Complimentarian philosophy. The complimentarian view simply stated, says that women and men can do some similar functions. However, they believe that there should still be a man in charge to oversee these functions. Based off of what I have studied in Scripture, this is an erroneous belief system.

As we study early texts and look further into history, we will see that the popular culture and followers of various religions were under the assumption that it was impossible for the female gender to function without any oversight or instruction from a man. This belief is still alive and well in today's society. For example, even something that's in popular culture today which many of you who are reading are very familiar with is the Duggar family. Almost everyone has read stories or watched them on the news or their television show. It's no secret they have a huge family are Christians; but one of the things that has been problematic even in recent times, is the fact that as the Duggar children began to become adults and the young women began to marry and have their own families, the media began to scrutinize their belief system in such a way that is irrational and ridiculous.

Here it is. The world, the secular society- that doesn't even believe in what the Duggar's have been taught regarding dress code, family structure, men being the head of women and ruling over them; Yet it has been found that in some of the articles concerning their family, the media has been largely negative in its scrutiny and assessment of what these young women do. For instance, when the young ladies started wearing pants, the first thing that was brought up was that their father taught them another way of living and that they should adhere to what their father said- but they did not. This, by implication made them look evil to the world. How could these young women be disobedient to their father? Shame on them! The news media posted a picture of these young women who were just starting out in their life-learning about their liberty, about what it meant to be a woman, this was all blown out of proportion by the criticisms of a world that didn't even possess the same belief system. How could their breaking of the dress code have offended people who were not adherents of the same? Now the media is painting a picture that these women are evil because of the fact that they are now branching out in life from under the supervision of their father (a man), and now they're wearing pants instead of just wearing dresses. And of course, this is also part of society's mentality that women should be veiled (As in Schmidt's book).

There are still misogynistic and base thoughts about how a woman should dress, how women should be thought of, and what liberty a woman should be allowed to have. It is so very important for us to understand that unless we deal with the mentality that is pervasive in our society, we will behave, respond, and even speak like the Pharisees of Jesus's Day. We may say that we believe that women should have liberty, but do we really examine our own prejudices? Those of us, especially women, sometimes we have fought within ourselves about what liberty's we should be allowed to have. There's always a struggle when it comes to rearing children. Being a wife, how much can you do? How much should you not be allowed to do, and then there's always that nagging thought, because of what we've been taught- that a wife has dreams, goals and a vision outside of her husband is nit submissive.

 The words, "wives should submit to their husbands"-That means to some people that a wife should have no say about anything. (I won't deal with submission too much in this chapter) however, I would like to bring to the forefront the mentality of our culture and the society in which we live. In so doing, I'm sure that it's going to be very easy to get an understanding of what women faced even during Jesus's time. It will also bring clarity to the importance and the power that is portrayed through Christs' engaging with women. It is so liberating. It is so powerful. It is so bondage-breaking that Jesus would touch a woman or let a woman touch him without demeaning her or making her feel like she is a social pariah. As theologians, we must gain the correct understanding of what Jesus's words actually meant. For how can we live in obedience to what is commanded concerning women, unless we actually understand what Jesus thought and taught about women?

It must not be forgotten that there were many women who traveled with Jesus as He went from town to town. They weren't merely part of the crowd. They were in the inner circle with Jesus; and although they were not called the twelve, they however, were inside the house with him. They were also given instruction even upon his resurrection directly from him to proclaim his resurrection.

His very contact with women and encountering them was counter cultural and liberating. I would like to share with you a quote from an Evangelical Bible Scholar, David Scholar,

> It is important to stress the inclusion of women in the group of Jesus's disciples, since the twelve have often been used in history of the church to argue that only men can exercise authority and leadership in the church. Jesus indicated clearly that discipleship was a higher priority than gender roles. Both Luke 8:19-21 (Mark 3:31-35; Matthew 12:46-50) and Luke 11:27-28 place obedience to the Word of God ABOVE the role of mother/motherhood. Thus, it is not surprising that Jesus' group of disciples included *women*.[12]

I love what Matthew 27:55 says, *"There were also many women there, looking on from a distance, who had followed Jesus from Galilee, ministering to him."*

That is phenomenal to see because he kept the women close to him. He allowed them to be a part of what he was doing. He allowed them to have a voice to participate even when men and culture disagreed.

I would like to insert a little caveat here about the fact that it is well understood that may churches do not teach this on the fact that Jesus liberated women. It is almost a taboo subject. In light of this lack of teaching the truth concerning this subject, in many cases in the past as well as today, women are not given equal privileges in Ministry or afforded the opportunities to operate in ministry. They have been omitted in part on a grand scale from the leadership roles within the church. It is safe to say and an accurate assumption, that many leaders in authority have not followed what Jesus taught through the scripture and through his life concerning the placement of the female gender in within the Christian community and society. And in doing so, there are many women who are within the church but they're angry. They are within the church, but they are frustrated because they feel as though they cannot exercise or complete the work that the Lord would have them to do.

I'm reminded of a time several years ago while when I was a young Believer. I visited one of the local assemblies. My husband was in the military at the time and we were acclimating to our new area. In so doing, I went looking for a church for us to be able to fellowship.

I happened upon a certain denominational church, which I actually knew nothing about, nor did I realize the stronghold that this particular religious group had in the area in which we lived. So, upon my attending the service, which was a very uplifting service; I noticed during worship that all the women sat on one side of the church and all the men sat on the other. It was odd to say the least, but then again, I was a young Believer and I wasn't really sure what that was about. Service concluded, and upon my exit, I was stopped as I attempted to leave the building. One of the female members of the church was inquiring about my possible return to the ministry, and whether I was going to come back and visit. I didn't see anything wrong with coming back to visit, so I affirmed that I had hoped to return again for another worship service. Once we conversed further, she asked if I would like to participate in one of their Home Bible Studies, and I thought to myself that would be excellent.

I'm a mom. I had small children at home. My husband is busy and he's in the military, so this will be a great asset to me to have someone that I can have a home Bible study with. So I thought. Needless to say, when the woman showed up to my home to conduct the Bible study session, one of the first things that she wanted to teach me was how the Scripture says that a woman is to be silent and that we as the female gender are the weaker vessels; as Help Meet for our husbands, our responsibility according to Scripture, is to follow our husband's lead in all things and not to usurp authority over him because he is the man and the "head".

I was able then to ask any questions that I had. I proceeded to make inquiry about the women sitting on opposite sides of the church from the men, and it was explained to me that it was for the purposes of purity so as not to cause any offense; and also to stave off any occasion for anyone to lust after the other. I know that sounds ridiculous. I thought so as well. However, as the Bible study ensued and she began to share different things about what she felt the scripture said and what she had been indoctrinated to believe in, I began to ask her even more questions. What if God has something for you to do, but your church teaches that you cannot do it because you have to be silent? What would you say to God? And of course, again, I'm a young believer, I'm in my early twenties at the time. I'm full of zeal and passion for the Lord. And though I came from the quintessential traditional pentecostal church where we are taught submission, as well as all those things she mentioned, I still could not wrap my mind around what this woman was saying to me.

It made absolutely no sense that God would save you and not only save you, but you have a testimony of the things that you have come through and that the only people that you could actually share that testimony with were other women; or you could teach the children. I knew from that point on that I wanted to end the Bible study and I did not want her to come back, not because I felt offended by what she had said, but I felt sorry for her. I felt as though she was bound. I felt as though she would never find her purpose because of what her church taught her. I know that when she left my house, she had several questions that she wanted to ask God herself, because I was insistent on her looking at the scripture and really looking again at what she thought was correct and not just taking her pastor's word for it.

That story always burns in my mind because of course, this church is still doing ministry in the area in which we live and they are still propagating the spiritual bondage of women. These are the kinds of ministries in this area that grow. It's unfortunate that we refuse to teach what Jesus taught about liberating women. Now mind you, we might like to call this "liberty" that I am referring to feminine or feminist theology, just like there are many others such as secular groups or religious groups that come up with their version of theology, but I must add, if Jesus has already taught about the liberation of women, why would women have to come up with another set of doctrines or philosophies or theology about their liberty? It's a moot point. There was no such thing as feminist theology. Why? Because the scripture already teaches that women are not have been made free in Christ and Jesus taught that women were equal to men in every way- be it what they offer naturally or what they bring to the table spiritually. So as we forge forward in this, it behooves us to really allow the words and the actions that Jesus took to sink in. We must allow God's word to get into our mindsets and into our spirit and allow it to break every bondage and falsehood that we have accepted. These molds have had an effect on our society. These mindsets are pervasive to such a degree that even those who are not Bible-believing Christians still have the mindset that women are to be subjugated. That is how heavy bondage is against women, and this mindset that a woman's worth is less than man's is an old paradigm that is in need of severe adjusting. It is imperative that we teach and preach what the Bible says and what Holy Spirit reveals. It is imperative that we, no matter how much flack we might receive from others, no matter how much rejection we receive from society, no matter how many denominations disagree or even scholars for that matter, that we stand on the truth of God's word. We must bear in mind that, just because they disagree, does not mean that we are incorrect. We know for a fact that Jesus was and is correct in his theology and in his presentation of how women should be treated, how women should be accepted, and what their status should look like in society.

I am sure the woman who had come to my house to lead this Bible study was no doubt she was frustrated by my non-conformist stance. It was so hard for her to let it sink into her or even fathom the idea that God would want to use her for a larger platform than just going house to house teaching Bible study to women. Mind you, I think that that was a great undertaking for her to even come and knock on my door and teach a Bible study. I thought that was a huge deal because it's a part of obeying the Great Commission and making disciples. It's great work. You're teaching the Gospel. However, she was limited in her ability of what she could do or who she could reach, because of what her denomination taught. I can imagine some of the issues that women in these types of denominations have had to face. I have on several occasions been the subject of criticism because of the fact that as a woman I'm preaching and teaching. I've been asked on occasion of preaching at a church concerning the message that I was going to preach that morning. I've personally been pulled into the office by a male Pastor, after accepting an engagement to preach- which he extended, and thoroughly interrogated about what my preaching texts were and what it was that I wanted to say to his congregation? I was flabbergasted. Why would you invite me to your church and then ask me what my message is before I preach? In my mind, I'm asking, do you do this to other guests who are not female? Upon getting to know this particular leader better, I learned that he has a serious problem with women in positions of authority in the church. He held to the Complimentarian view that women could lead, but only under the watchful eye and supervision of a male spiritual leader. Of course, this made me feel less than. It caused much frustration for me and I can imagine how some other women may feel being a part of denominations or within organizations that treat them as though as a woman, they have no value, substance or authority without a man. It is sad to be made to feel as though women should just settle and be satisfied with what measure of respect she receives, if any; even if it is less than what a man receives. This kind of thinking also causes us to be passive in some instances or overly aggressive, because it is difficult to share your gifts and walk in the fullness of them in the midst of people who are supposed to believe like you believe, yet they don't-and not because you are ill-qualified, but solely based upon the fact that you have been born a woman.

Unbeknownst to these false teachers, they are just like the men, the Pharisees and the teachers of Jesus' time who believed that women should have no voice or at the very least, if you do have a voice, there should be a limitation on what you are allowed to share and with whom you may share it. It's unfortunate that many women in ministry face issues like this because they are manipulated into believing that God will only use them in a certain way. Not only are they manipulated into believing the aforementioned- but they are also manipulated into believing that if they try to do anything outside of what has been given to them, then you are labeled Jezebels. They are considered a Delilah, some kind of seductress-they are labeled rebellious.

These leaders make women feel as if they don't really want to hear from God about fulfilling ministry because they don't want to submit to someone that will stifle their purpose. And these are the things we want to shatter because it is high time we embraced Truth. We must study, receive and not just receive it, but make it part of our personal belief system. What Jesus taught and what we see in the Scripture must be received as Truth.

I would like to share with you a little snippet from a friend and mentor of mine who wrote in an outstanding book: "10 Things Jesus Taught About Women: And A Few Things He Didn't Teach." This is from a chapter that is called, "Men and Are Women Equal."

> When we understand the prevailing thinking about women in Jesus's Day, we begin to understand how radical His teaching was. We begin to see what He was up against.
>
> ❖ The oral law of Jesus's day said: let the words with the Law be burned rather than committed to women... If a

man teaches his daughter the Law, it is as though he taught her lewdness. (Sotah3:4)

❖ A woman is inferior to her husband in all things. Let her, therefore, be obedient to him. (Apion 2:25).

❖ Let a curse come upon the man who must needs must needs have his wife or children say grace for him.

❖ Praise be to God that He is not created me a Gentile; Praise be to God that He created me not a woman; Praise be to God that He has not created me an ignorant man. (This is a Jewish thanksgiving prayer of Jesus day from Menahot 43b)

❖ It is well for those whose children are male, but ill for those whose children are female…. At the birth of a boy, all are joyful, but at the birth of a girl all are sad…. When a boy comes into the world, peace comes into the world; When a girl comes, nothing comes…. Even the most virtuous of women is a witch (Niddah 31b)

When we become aware of social practices regarding women in Jesus's day, we gain further insight into the revolutionary nature of his teaching.

❖ In the Jerusalem temple, women were limited to one outer portion, the women's court, which was five steps below the court for men.

❖ A Rabbi regarded it beneath his dignity to speak to a woman in public.

❖ Women were kept for child-bearing and rearing, and they were always under the strict control of a man.

These prevailing thoughts and social practices reflect the sinful nature of humanity resulting from the fall. They also reveal how the thinking of God's Chosen People had been corrupted by syncretism with pink pagan cultures.

When we read the Gospels with knowledge, we understand that the writers clearly show us that Jesus rejected the idea that women are evil, inferior, unclean, and an equal. Nowhere do the gospel writers portray women as being of lesser value than men. Nowhere are women restricted to certain roles, and nowhere are women treated as the property

of men or subjects under male authority. Instead, Jesus, our
Lord, demonstrated most vigorously that women and men
are equal.[13]

That is a powerful, powerful writing. It is so essential that we look into
the Scripture, that we study what we see in Scripture, and that we study
what has been presented; the lifestyle, the words of Jesus, and how he
engaged with other women, so that we will know what He actually taught
concerning women. Our denominational practices are not of great
importance. What Jesus actually taught – that is what is of greatest
importance.

Here are some verses for you to study in your free time that show how
Jesus dealt with women: John 8:3-11. We see Jesus dealing with Mary and
Martha in Luke 10:38-42; The woman at the well: John 4:4-26; and Mary
Magdalen in Matthew 27:55-57.

6

SHATTERING PERCEPTIONS

'Like fish, we "swim" in a sea of images, and these images help shape our perceptions of the world and of ourselves.' (Berger, 2008)

We will begin this subject by first looking into the Scripture.
John chapter 8:3 says, "the scribes and the Pharisees brought a woman who had been caught in adultery," Isn't it funny they bring the woman who was caught in adultery, but where was the man? " and placing her in the midst they said to him, teacher this woman has been caught in the act of adultery. Now in the law of Moses commanded us to stone such women. so what do you say? This they said to test him that they may have some charge to bring against him. Jesus bent down and wrote with his finger on the ground. And as they as they continued to ask him, he stood up and said to him to them, let him who is without sin among you be the first to throw a stone at her. And once more he bent down and wrote on the ground. But when they heard it, they went away one by one, beginning with the older ones and Jesus was left alone with the woman standing before him. Jesus stood up and said to her, 'woman where are they? Has no one condemned you? She said no one, Lord. And Jesus said, neither do I condemn you; go, and from now on sin no more."

Look at what Jesus was doing in vss. 3-11. You have to understand that not only was Jesus forgiving stand for God to forgive sin that is not a big deal because that is his nature to forgive. God is a forgiving God, but what Jesus was doing? He was shattering perceptions about women. He was shattering the mindsets of what the people thought about women in that day.

It is ironic how this all unfolds. With all the that's going on in the church-world these days- such as women becoming Bishops and Apostles, (myself included.) The whole woman question coming up again, doesn't surprise me. I had just finish teaching (I was teaching two classes), and we had just finished our second week, In our second week of classes, we discussed the subject of women in authority, apostolic women and women in ministry.

I was also teaching about the issues that surround the woman question. I was in disbelief when I was approached about this again. My thought was, "are you kidding me? Are we back at this again?"

I'm fully aware that this issue has been going on in the church for centuries. My dilemma began when I listened to a very prominent minister who was born again and trained for ministry by a female pastor, stand and denounce women in ministry! It's unbelievable! How could you possibly denounce women being pastors and leaders when you were born again in a church lead by a woman? It makes no sense to me! However, this leader was allowed to make this claim and no one call him on the carpet about his erroneous doctrine. My question to that particular minister who now decries women in ministry would be, was your salvation experience real? What about all the things that you were taught in that ministry growing up? Can you believe those things? How did you once believe something and now that you have a major platform, you denounce your former belief to the detriment of those women who are now following your ministry?

He is clearly contradicting himself without really realizing what he is doing. Every one of us needs to learn the art of becoming theologians because we are studying the scripture that is our responsibility- that we might be able to give an answer to every man for the faith that lies in us.

Now, let's get back to my first point. Jesus is shattering perceptions. Notice what it says in the 31st verse of this chapter: "if you do what I say, if you follow my words, then you are my disciples." Then he said, "if you abide in me and if you abide in my word, you are truly my disciples; and you will know the truth and the truth will make you free." That means that these believers thought they knew the truth, but what they. believed was not truth at all! Jesus said, they would know the truth, when you know what the truth is, it is going to make you free! Jesus had to shatter the perception that women were unclean, evil, and inferior. Clearly, that is what they believed, but is could not be further from the truth!

Jesus was shattering this perception! Now the fact that he was even speaking to this woman is a major event. And we are also aware of the fact that the woman didn't commit adultery by herself ...where was this man she had been with? We all understand that the man who participated in the sin with the woman mentioned in the verses that we read should have been present to face his accusers and receive judgment as well. This fact made room for Jesus to deal with the perceptions of the culture. These men thought that women were evil and unclean or else they wouldn't have been prepared to deal with her in such an unjust manner.

This was the pervasive thought pattern that permeated throughout the culture. You cannot receive an accurate understanding of the Scriptures by doing a surface study of the verses we've read. You must include in your study, the historicity of the Scriptures when you read in the Bible. We must note the context of the text in question. A good rule of thumb to remember is text out of context no text at all. The next item to consider is the pretext. These must all be taken into account when seeking understanding of Scripture. The fact that many draw conclusions without following the steps above, is the reason we find so many erroneous doctrines that have been adopted by the church. When you go to Bible College, you have to study Manners and Customs. If you've never studied Manners and Customs of the Bible, please take a minute and go to the library and get the book. Look it up online. You can get a copy of Manners and Customs of the Bible from any bookstore and be able to decipher the traditions.

This brings me to another point. Jesus was shattering traditions and beliefs that taught that the woman was responsible for many of the wicked things that were taking place. When I hear people talking and they go back to the book of Genesis and they say. "the Bible says that Eve sinned first." My response is, the curse didn't come just because she sinned. The curse was pronounced because both Adam and Eve sinned. God's creation sinned and because of that, they both suffered the consequences. If the woman was not responsible for anything, and her position inconsequential, there would have been no reason for God to make her suffer judgment of the curse along with Adam. It's a simple deduction! You don't have to be a scholar to come to the conclusion that only responsible parties are held accountable for their actions. If Eve's (the woman's) position is so much lessor in value, power, position and authority, why wasn't she absolved of her wrong-doing and only Adam held accountable for transgression of God's commandment? That's a good question, isn't it? It's because they both (Adam and Eve) were given dominion and ruled equally in the Garden of Eden and therefore, they were jointly and individually guilty of transgressing -which meant they both were to be punished EQUALLY!

If what I have stated above is not the case, and if woman is indeed inferior to man, then she should not be held accountable for the choice she made, nor should she have faced being cursed. The truth is that God was showing that even in His pronouncing judgment on them both, that women were equal in substance, equal in authority and value.

Let's look at this in the book of Matthew. You need to read this for yourself. Before we look at the verses, please understand, Jesus lived in a "man's world." This was what is called a Patriarchal Society. This means that men were in authority over women in every aspect of life and function. Not only so, but women were thought of as property and didn't have the same rights, privileges and authority as men. Women who lived during the period of time when Scripture was written, in fact, had no voice. However, as you read the Gospels, you will see that woven throughout the Scripture, Jesus gave women a voice; even though it was not an acceptable practice.

To add a quick side-bar note; I want to bring into the picture Feminism and what it really is and where it originated. The best thing to do is to begin with a dictionary and to define what Feminism is. So let's start there. *[3]Feminism-the advocacy of women's rights on the basis of the equality of the sexes.* The reason we need to unearth this terminology is due to the fact that many Believers are under the assumption that Feminism and the Feminist movement originates from some demonically inspired individual. In fact, the Women's Suffrage Movement was spearheaded by Believing women who stood against the injustices that were committed against them, solely because of their gender. Prophetically, we are still here and this issue, though not as harsh as it once was, still needs addressing so we turn to the Scripture so that we can learn from Jesus as he elevates women and shatters the prevailing perceptions of that era by speaking to them, giving them commands, forgiving their sins, allowing them to be His followers and defending them even when they have been caught in sin by the very men that sought to keep them subservient.

It is of utmost importance, as I have already stated, that we understand the historicity, pretext, context, and post-text of the Scripture so that we are able to read and understand accurately what is being stated, to whom it is stated and how it should be interpreted. The Bible instructs us to *"Study to show thyself approved unto God, a workman that needeth not to be ashamed, rightly dividing the word of truth.: (2 Tim 2:15, KJV)* Now that we have dealt with that, we can finally go to Matthew as planned.

Look at Matthew 9:20-22; *"And behold, a woman who had suffered discharged of blood for twelve years came up behind Him and touched the fringe of His garment, for she said to herself, "If I only touch His garment, I will be made well." Jesus turned, and seeing her He said, "Take heart, daughter, your faith has made you well." And instantly, the woman was made well."*

What was Jesus doing here in the verses we just read? First of all, this woman, who was already deemed unclean according to the Law, risked her very life-crawling through the thronging crowd to touch Jesus for her healing. Not only was she already ceremonially unclean, she contaminated every person in the crowd she pushed against in her pursuit of healing! If they had known that this unclean vessel was in their midst, purposely defiling others just to get to Jesus, they would have most certainly had her stoned! Now, seeing this through the eyes of a Hebrew people, who knew the Law and some in the crowd who no doubt knew the medical history of this woman, Jesus proceeds to 1. Speak to her, and 2. heal her instead of rebuking her and having her immediately brought to judgment for stoning!

Now, back to the question at hand, what was Jesus doing? The obvious answer is that He was healing the woman with the issue of blood. More importantly, if we look deeper into the facts that have been previously shared before we read this text, we will see the real motive and power behind the gesture toward this woman. For those reading this who are nor well-versed with the Law of Moses, this woman was considered "unclean", (Leviticus 15:19); So again, what was Jesus doing when He healed this woman? He was removing the perception that women were unclean! When Jesus forgave the woman caught in adultery, He was making a statement and delivering her from the cultural perception that women were evil! (John 8:1-11). Jesus deliberately did these miracles in public to heal the societal perceptions that prevailed during that time and to show them openly that He was a champion for women; that the new way He was introducing, though new to them, showed the love, compassion and care God has for women and that femininity was to be celebrated, not bashed and shunned.

The importance of this is far beyond one culture. Our perceptions, even today, must be adjusted due to the fact that what we perceive dictates how or if we are able to receive. So, if women are to be treated as second class citizens, how then can she carry the Gospel and bring glory to God? How then can she start a business and even dream of being slightly successful when she is already frowned upon at the threshold of the door of opportunity? It is impossible! Therefore, it is of utmost urgency that we navigate through the Scripture with proper perspective and look deeper than our commentaries to see the heart of our Lord and interpret His actions in such a way that we are able to see the great revelation that is hidden behind His every action as He lifted, praised, encouraged and released the woman from the bondages of faulty perceptions of the men in the society in which she lived.

It is noteworthy to add that there is a direct correlation between the perceptions of women and how society receives from them, and even the result of how females will view themselves as women. It is impossible to separate the ideologies of a culture from the behavior and perceptions that are born as a result of them. Culture has the power to influence every facet of our lives; thoughts, behaviors, dress codes and it even determines what we deem as acceptable and normal as a people. Hence, the message and ministry of Jesus, as a counter-cultural hammer, swinging in polar-opposite of the socially acceptable norms; freeing women from the bondage of the pasts short-sighted and prejudicial chains.

If we are to properly raise sons as well as daughters with a healthy understanding and appreciation of women and womanhood, we must first pull down the strongholds that yet prevail; not only in archaic societies, or third-world countries who seem behind the times, but also, right here in the United States of America- in the year 2017! There is still a struggle and overarching thought that has intermingled with modern culture and beliefs today. These beliefs state that women are in some way inferior or unequal to men and that this one gender of humanity is the purveyor of many of the woes of our society.

We see it in television programs every day. Women are portrayed as witches-even to our children (Disney's Cruella D'Ville); or they are the quintessential housewife who looks perfect on the outside, yet she is a wonton seductress who seeks sexual gratification outside her marriage covenant, (ABC's Desperate Housewives).

Our responsibility as Believers is to search the Word of God for the Truth and to share it with others that they may walk in liberty, continuing the ministry that Jesus began. As we faithfully do our part and teach others, we too, will shatter the perceptions in our society by answering the woman question.

7

IN SEARCH OF A SMURF..MAN

Chris: I get it! So [points to Danny] you're the cool one, [points to Wallow] you're the funny one, [points to Beth] and you're the....

Beth: Girl.

— Bravest Warriors, "Memory Donk"[1]

This entire chapter is a necessary read. While doing my research, I came across so many informative articles, blogs and historical texts that it was almost impossible to choose what would be used as resources. Women's rights and its history are a vast subject matter, with many winding turns. You will notice that there are a great many block quotes within this chapter. The reason, there is no need to reinvent the wheel. The things I felt the necessity to pen on my own, that was done- as I have years of study from my college days and many of my written works have been used within this study guide. There are other things, however, that have been stated so articulately and carried so much weight, that the only way to ensure proper use of what I had read and to do this written work any justice, was to allow either some or parts of the researched articles to stand on their own merit and allow the powerful words that I read to be transferred for others in their entirety to read. Of course, the integrity of every contributor's work is attributed to them for the sake of intellectual integrity.

As you are reading, I challenge you to peruse the bibliography and read the plethora of resources listed. Your understanding will be enriched, and you just may learn a little something that you did not previously know.

The Smurfette Principle is in action when the cast is made up of a group of males and exactly one female. This can occur even in works with loads and loads of characters, so long as each sub-ensemble (of five or more) contains only one female character. Adding a second female to the ensemble creates a related trope. With the relatively few female-aimed works, contrasting the sheer volume of works that are aimed at males, it stands out that the demographics of fiction shows a ratio of female to male characters much lower than real life.

Albeit being named after Smurfette from The Smurfs, the name of this trope was first coined by an article by Katha Pollitt in the New York Times printed April 7, 1991, called "The Smurfette Principle". The article focused on the trope as it applies to young children and discussed the negative message: males are individuals who have adventures, while females are a type of deviation who exist only in relation to males. See also Margaret McGowan's Reel Girl column Females 51% of population but minority of imaginary characters and real- life power positions.

Compare (the following articles which are available online): The Bechdel Test, Two Girls to a Team, and Two Guys and a Girl for similar critiques of female-male proportions in fiction. See Chromosome Casting when there's zero members of the opposite sex present in the work. This is also Distaff Counterpart to The One Guy. Subtropes include Never a Self-Made Woman (women cannot achieve anything without a male mentor or counterpart), Smurfette Breakout (the Smurfette character becomes popular on her own), Starring Smurfette (Smurfette is the protagonist), and Territorial Smurfette (another female is added to the show and the original Smurfette reacts negatively). Contrast (also articles under the following subjects): Gender-Equal Ensemble and Improbably Female Cast. For the music equivalent, you would have a male band and a female singer.[1]

Take a look at the kids' section of your local video store. You'll find that features starring boys, and usually aimed at them, account for 9 out of 10 offerings. Clicking the television dial one recent week -- admittedly not an encyclopedic study -- I came across not a single network cartoon or puppet show starring a female. (Nickelodeon, the children's cable channel, has one of each.) Except for the crudity of the animation and the general air of witlessness and hype, I might as well have been back in my own 1950's childhood, nibbling Frosted Flakes in front of Daffy Duck, Bugs Bunny, Porky Pig and the rest of the all-male Warner Brothers lineup.

Contemporary shows are either essentially all-male, like "Garfield," or are organized on what I call the Smurfette principle: a group of male buddies will be accented by a lone female, stereotypically defined. In the worst cartoons -- the ones that blend seamlessly into the animated cereal commercials -- the female is usually a little-sister type, a bunny in a pink dress and hair ribbons who tags along with the adventurous bears and badgers. But the Smurfette principle rules the more carefully made shows, too. Thus, Kanga, the only female in "Winnie-the-Pooh," is a mother. Piggy, of "Muppet Babies," is a pint-size version of Miss Piggy, the camp glamour queen of the Muppet movies. April, of the wildly popular "Teen-Age Mutant Ninja Turtles," functions as a girl Friday to a quartet of male superheroes. The message is clear. Boys are the norm, girls the variation; boys are central, girls peripheral; boys are individuals, girls types. Boys define the group, its story and its code of values. Girls exist only in relation to boys.

Well, commercial television -- what did I expect? The surprise is that public television, for all its superior intelligence, charm and commitment to worthy values, shortchanges preschool girls, too. Mister Rogers lives in a neighborhood populated mostly by middle-aged men like himself. "Shining Time Station" features a cartoon in which the male characters are train engines and the female characters are passenger cars. And then there's "Sesame Street." True, the human characters are neatly divided between the genders (and among the races, too, which is another rarity). The film clips, moreover, are just about the only place on television in which you regularly see girls having fun together: practicing double Dutch, having a sleep-over. But the Muppets are the real stars of "Sesame Street," and the important ones -- the ones with real personalities, who sing on the musical videos, whom kids identify with and cherish in dozens of licensed products -- are all male. I know one little girl who was so outraged and heartbroken when she realized that even Big Bird -- her last hope -- was a boy that she hasn't watched the show since.

Well, there's always the library. Some of the best children's books ever written have been about girls -- Madeline, Frances the badger. It's even possible to find stories with funny, feminist messages, like "The Paperbag Princess." (She rescues the prince from a dragon, but he's so ungrateful that she decides not to marry him, after all.) But books about girls are a subset in a field that includes a much larger subset of books about boys (12 of the 14 storybooks singled out for praise in last year's Christmas roundup in Newsweek, for instance) and books in which the sex of the child is theoretically unimportant -- in which case it usually "happens to be" male. Dr. Seuss's books are less about individual characters than about language and imaginative freedom -- but, somehow or other, only boys get to go on beyond Zebra or see marvels on Mulberry Street. Frog and Toad, Lowly Worm, Lyle the Crocodile, all could have been female. But they're not.

Do kids pick up on the sexism in children's culture? You bet. Preschoolers are like medieval philosophers: the text -- a book, a movie, a TV show -- is more authoritative than the evidence of their own eyes. "Let's play weddings," says my little niece. We grownups roll our eyes, but face it: it's still the one scenario in which the girl is the central figure. "Women are nurses ," my friend Anna, a doctor, was informed by her then 4-year-old, Molly. Even my Sophie is beginning to notice the back-seat role played by girls in some of her favorite books. "Who's that?" she asks every time we reread "The Cat in the Hat." It's Sally, the timid little sister of the resourceful boy narrator. She wants Sally to matter, I think, and since Sally is really just a name and a hair ribbon, we have to say her name again and again.

The sexism in preschool culture deforms both boys and girls. Little girls learn to split their consciousness, filtering their dreams and ambitions through boy characters while admiring the clothes of the princess. The more privileged and daring can dream of becoming exceptional women in a man's world -- Smurfettes. The others are being taught to accept the more usual fate, which is to be a passenger car drawn through life by a masculine train engine. Boys, who are rarely confronted with stories in which males play only minor roles, learn a simpler lesson: girls just don't matter much.

How can it be that 25 years of feminist social change have made so little impression on preschool culture? Molly, now 6 and well aware that women can be doctors, has one theory: children's entertainment is mostly made by men. That's true, as it happens, and I'm sure it explains a lot. It's also true that, as a society, we don't seem to care much what goes on with kids, as long as they are reasonably quiet. Marshmallow cereal, junky toys, endless hours in front of the tube -- a society that accepts all that is not going to get in a lather about a little gender stereotyping. It's easier to focus on the bright side. I had "Cinderella," Sophie has "The Little Mermaid" -- that's progress, isn't it?

"We're working on it," Dulcy Singer, the executive producer of "Sesame Street," told me when I raised the sensitive question of those all-male Muppets. After all, the show has only been on the air for a quarter of a century; these things take time. The trouble is, our preschoolers don't have time. My funny, clever, bold, adventurous daughter is forming her gender ideas right now. I do what I can to counteract the messages she gets from her entertainment, and so does her father -- Sophie watches very little television. But I can see we have our work cut out for us. It sure would help if the bunnies took off their hair ribbons, and if half of the monsters were fuzzy, blue -- and female.[2]

3

Everybody knew you as the wife of a famous man,

Everybody who knew said, "There goes Dixon's girl again."

— Dessa, "Dixon's Girl"[4]

This is an insidious trope where a female character's success is undermined by the narrative of a male character providing advantages necessary for them. She's usually framed as someone's sister, girlfriend or love interest. And if she's a military or political leader of some sort, then you can bet that she got the position with help from her father or another male relative. The story implies her membership is due to motivation and training by her powerful male relatives who are active on the same field. In short, a personal, emotional relationship with a mentor is needed, not just a professional one driven by her own independent ambitions.

82

This character stands in contrast to Self-Made Man, where a character (usually male, but not always) was able to accomplish goals well beyond their advantages. In short, this is another example of Double Standard. Due to stereotypes about separate gender roles, writers will often use this trope to justify to viewers (presumed male) why they should care about the female character at all, as it is assumed the female character would not have taken an interest had it not been for the presence of that male character.

Going hand with this is Men Act, Women Are, which is about what comes from the man, and where the woman comes from. Compare Lineage Comes from the Father, which deals with bloodlines. I Have Brothers is a more mild version of this trope that nonetheless associates a woman's less traditionally feminine interests with a male influence rather than her own volition.

Keep in mind that this is not the strict inverse of Self-Made Woman and does not apply to every instance of a female character being helped by a male friend, relative, or love interest to reach her position. Rather, the male character must be implied to be more important to the plot or setting than the female character is, and the main force responsible for her position (e.g. the token female of the squad is a skilled soldier, but she's introduced as "the general's daughter" first and foremost, whereas her male companions aren't defined in the same way).[4]

8

SEX KITTENS

OR

WOMEN OF VIRTUE

There is no other way to address this except by being very direct because there seems to be a dilemma in the church and in the world today. We have lost the desire to be virtuous women in exchange for a Hollywood persona. The world is not the only one driven by high-fashion and commercials that tell us we need to buy everything we see, because "we need it." The church, namely, women in the church have been seduced and overtaken by commercialism and blatant sexual prowess.

Let's begin by reading the following verses:

Proverbs 31:10-31 (KJV)

Who can find a virtuous woman? for her price is far above rubies. The heart of her husband doth safely trust in her, so that he shall have no need of spoil. She will do him good and not evil all the days of her life. She seeketh wool, and flax, and worketh willingly with her hands. She is like the merchants' ships; she bringeth her food from afar. She riseth also while it is yet night, and giveth meat to her household, and a portion to her maidens. She considereth a field, and buyeth it: with the fruit of her hands she planteth a vineyard. She girdeth her loins with strength, and strengtheneth her arms. She perceiveth that her merchandise is good: her candle goeth not out by night. She layeth her hands to the spindle, and her hands hold the distaff. She stretcheth out her hand to the poor; yea, she reacheth forth her hands to the needy. She is not afraid of the snow for her household: for all her household are clothed with scarlet. She maketh herself coverings of tapestry; her clothing is silk and purple. Her husband is known in the gates, when he sitteth among the elders of the land. She maketh fine linen, and selleth it; and delivereth girdles unto the merchant. Strength and honour are her clothing; and she shall rejoice in time to come. She openeth praised.Give her of the fruit of her hands; and let her own works her mouth with wisdom; and in her tongue is the law of kindness. She looketh well to the ways of her household, and eateth not the bread of idleness. Her children arise up, and call her blessed; her husband also, and he praiseth her.Many daughters have done virtuously, but thou excellest them all. Favour is deceitful, and beauty is vain: but a woman that feareth the Lord, she shall be praise her in the gates.

Faulty Reality

We have pews full of women, but we can't say that they all are virtuous. Unfortunately, we have a problem with watching too much reality television. Reality television really isn't our reality; it's someone else's reality. Here it is, Solomon is being spoken to by his mother, Bathsheba. She is telling him what to look out for because she knew the type of woman she once was. She remembered all too well what happened as result of her bathing on top of her house in the morning when everybody was at home. She understood what she needed to tell her children. Isn't it true that we know how to tell our sons and daughters what to look for in a companion?

When we look in our churches, we are finding out that the women in the church are acting like the Real Housewives of Atlanta. We have a problem in that this is what the world is putting out there, and we don't have sense enough not to repeat it. If Solomon is being asked who can find a virtuous woman, this means that virtuous women are not found as often as we need to find them. We are preoccupied with other things. It is unfortunate that some of us will go to church and shout and dance after we just left the club or jumped out of someone else's bed. We will come to church after we just finished hugging up or smooching with someone we had no business hugging up or smooching with. We do all of that and then want to come to church and call ourselves virtuous. Not so.

First of all, she says to him that "her price is far above rubies." You can't even put a price on a real virtuous woman. Her value exceeds that which you can pay for. When you find a real good woman, you can't buy her. It doesn't matter how many cars you have or how much money you have. It doesn't matter if you try to take her to dinner or take her to some fancy hotel because you want to try to get your groove on or whatever - none of that is going to allow her to lose her virtue. Now I know you know what I'm talking about. If you don't, just pray for me. Verse eleven says that *"The heart of her husband doth safely trust in her, so that he shall have no need of spoil."* Our husbands should know that they can trust in us. If you are married, Jesus is your husband, and He should be able to trust you. This means that you should not be laying down with anyone that you are not married to. It means that you are going to be saved when you come to church and saved when you walk out the door. When I leave the house, my husband isn't worried about where I'm going. He's not having to ring my phone and ask me where I am and who I'm with. He doesn't have a fear of me smooching up with somebody else. He knows what he's got. Our husbands should know what they have. Those of you who aren't married need to know that God knows what He's got in you. You should be able to carry yourself as a godly woman.

Wanton Women

Let's talk about a few things concerning godly women. We have to learn how to cover some things up. Even concerning the mothers, we don't know if they are mothers or what they are because of how they are dressed. We come to church and the mothers of the church are trying to pick up the young men in the church. We've got cougars in the church, and that makes no sense! We can't trust our young men in the church because Mother So & So is trying to pick them up. Mother is wearing her skirts as short as she can wear them, and her chest is hanging out. That's not right! You should be able to be trusted. Can anyone trust you? Can we trust you to be a mother? It's the truth anyhow. I've seen it. It's enough to make you sick. This is still the gospel anyway. Even if people don't want it to be preached. It's the truth anyhow. God said that His house shall be called the house of prayer, but we have made it a den of thieves (Matthew 21:23). Some people aren't stealing money, but they are stealing the hearts and the souls of men.

Verse twelve says that *"She will do him good and not evil all the days of her life."* Though my husband gets on my nerves, I'm not going do him any evil. I'm not going to engage in wickedness to get back at him. I might think about it but I'm going to rebuke it. Don't act like you're so sanctified that you don't think about getting back at folks. You know that's the truth! Verse thirteen says that *"She seeketh wool, and flax, and worketh willingly with her hands."* She's not a lazy woman. There's nothing worse than being lazy. Nobody can rely on you because you're lazy. We call your house at 1:00 in the afternoon and you're still in the bed? You're lazy. We have to learn how to get up out of the bed and be about our Father's business. This is talking about a woman who finds a way to do what she needs to do and as a result, her husband will be praised. It's hard for some of us to do something for someone else to get the glory for all of our hard work. How do you feel when you do something and someone else gets the credit? We feel slighted. We like to receive our little applause.

An Industrious Woman

The Bible says in the fourteenth and fifteenth verses that "She is like the merchants' ships; she bringeth her food from afar. She riseth also while it is yet night, and giveth meat to her household, and a portion to her maidens." I told you that she's not in the bed at 1:00pm. We have to be industrious. It is the will of God that we as women learn how to make good use of our time. Instead of us being on the phone and Facebooking all day long, we need to be using our time to do the will of God. I'm sure that God deals with all of us about making sure that we have time in prayer, time in the word, time to take care of what needs to be taken care of at home, and time for ministry. You have to have time for these things, and you can't do that if you're in the bed all day. Now don't get me wrong: I have days in which I sleep in. I'm not saying that you can't have a day to sleep in. I'm not saying that you can't have a chill day. But every day can't be your chill day. You can't have so many chill days that you don't even know what day it is.

Verses sixteen and seventeen tell us that *"She considereth a field, and buyeth it: with the fruit of her hands she planteth a vineyard. She girdeth her loins with strength, and strengtheneth her arms."* I need to tell you that there's not always going to be someone to come along and speak strength to you. You're going to have to learn how to speak strength to yourself. You're going to have to learn to strengthen your own arm. You will have to learn how to speak life to yourself when you feel like you're dying or already dead. Strength is her girdle. It's what holds her together. When she feels like falling apart when life is getting on her nerves, and when it seems like all hell is breaking loose, she has something on the inside of her that's helping her to stay and stand. It used to be that praying women had some stamina about themselves. You wouldn't see strong women of God backsliding every five minutes. I know we go through and I know we have circumstances that come against us. I know that there are things we must experience, but can you stay saved for forty-eight hours? Can you hold on to

Jesus for more than an hour of service so that when you leave, we don't have to have prayer with you again?

Verse eighteen says, "*She perceiveth that her merchandise is good: her candle goeth not out by night.*" I don't need you to come and tell me that what I made is good. You don't need your neighbor to come and tell you that what you made is good. You should already know it's good,, and you should be industrious and go make money from it. It used to be that women would do whatever they had to do so that their families would be able to make it. Where are those women today? They wouldn't let the sun go down before they handled their business. While everybody else is in the bed and going to sleep, the virtuous woman is seeking the Lord. She's trying to find out what God wants her to do. She's asking God for instruction and direction. Where are the women who are intercessors that will get on their faces before the Lord? Where are the women who will burn the midnight oil? It's alright for us to come to church and look cute. I like my makeup, my high heels and all of that, but there has to be more to us than that. I believe that this life we are living is going to require that we have more than a cute face and a pair of pumps. You'd better have something in your inner man. You'd better have some strength in your girdle. You'd better be able to take something. You have to know how to go through and endure. You have to be able to pray through. Even if you feel like giving up, you'd better not give up.

We learn in verses nineteen and twenty that *"She layeth her hands to the spindle, and her hands hold the distaff. She stretcheth out her hand to the poor; yea, she reacheth forth her hands to the needy."* In other words, she's not just concerned about "me, my, and mine". Her heart is on those who are in need. She's not selfish. She's not just concerned about making herself and her family only. She's a good neighbor. Once upon a time we had some godly women who were good neighbors. I should be concerned about my sister who's sitting next to me. She shouldn't even have to tell me what's going on, because I should be sensitive enough in the spirit to pick her up. You have to have your mind on somebody other than you in order for that to happen. She stretches out her hand to the poor. When's the last time that you were at the store and you saw that someone didn't have enough money, so you gave them the extra that they needed to be able to pay for their bill? When's the last time you felt led to give someone some money for gas while they were standing at the counter, whether they had enough or not. A virtuous woman is not just concerned about herself and what she can do for herself. She's not just concerned about making sure she has food in her house, gas in her car, and necessities for her kids. She's looking out for her neighbor. Look out for your neighbor Virtuous Woman!

We already know that we as women have 900 things on our lists. I do too - I probably have 920 and you probably have 922. We have to learn how to balance all of that. We must learn how to be what God has called us to be. There is no excuse for you not to fulfill what God has given you to do. We can make up excuses all we want to, but God isn't hearing them. He isn't receiving any of our many excuses. You need to believe that. You can go to God with your excuses if you want to. It's not that this is a to-do list of things that God wants you to do. You know what God wants you to do because you feel it by conviction. We feel by conviction what God wants us to do, and when we're not doing it, our conscience condemns us for our disobedience.

I can't really read this verse for those who dwell in the warmer regions of our country, but verse twenty-one says that *"She is not afraid of the snow for her household: for all her household are clothed with scarlet."* Virtuous women aren't worried about a storm coming because they prepare for the storm. The Bible says that a prudent man sees the storm approaching and prepares himself (Proverbs 22:3). This virtuous woman is just that way. She can go outside and just tell that the storm is coming, and she'll go ahead and get her house ready. These are the craziest times we have ever lived in, and some of these women don't have a clue about anything. They're cute but they're crazy. Some of them are as dumb as a bag of rocks. They can't boil water. They can't make a pot of rice without a rice cooker. Question: How are you from down south and you can't cook rice without a rice cooker? You want a husband, but you can't cook. No man wants to eat KFC every night. No man wants McDonald's and Burger King every night. Mothers used to teach the younger women how to cook if they didn't know how. They used to prepare young women to be wives. It doesn't matter if the mothers are only thirty - if that's what God put in the house, and they know how to make some rice and clean a house, you'd better sit down and listen to them. I'm not saying that cooking is all you need to know how to do, but you still need to know how to do it. You need to have something that you're bringing to the table. If you can't cook and brother can't cook, how are y'all gonna eat?

During the time of my first wedding anniversary, we were waiting for housing at Fort Dix. My husband volunteered to cook some dinner for me, and I was so excited. He went in the kitchen and fried some chicken - I can't remember what else he cooked because I couldn't get over the chicken. That's all I remember is the chicken. We sat down at the table and that chicken was beautiful! It was nice and brown and crispy. When I broke that chicken open, it just ran with blood. I shouted, "Oh my God! Let me go fix this." I give him credit because at least he tried. He can cook now, but back then...not so much! And if I didn't know how to cook, there would have been no celebration. We would have both been looking at each other crazy trying to figure out what we were going to eat.

Don't be afraid of the snow or of the storm that's coming. Be prepared. Stop waiting until the last minute for everything. Some of us are last-minute planners. We wait down until the last minute. Church starts at the same time every Sunday. Why haven't you set your clock? Why didn't you get gas the night before? You know you're supposed to be in place. I'm talking about being a virtuous woman. Most work schedules begin the same time every day. That means you need to take care of your responsibilities-that may include ensuring that dinner and home taken care of. Where is your preparation? Prepare yourself. What if your household is dependent on you, and you're out of place? What if you forget? What if you wait until the last minute? You can't do that and inthe end, your home not suffer the consequences as a result.

Modesty is Not Outdated

Verse twenty-two says that "*She maketh herself coverings of tapestry; her clothing is silk and purple.*" She has her body covered up. It's funny how we sit on the front row of the church and try to pull our hem line down. Baby, there isn't any more material there. You can't pull anything else. There's nothing left for you to pull. Get you a lap cloth or get you a longer skirt. I'm not trying to take you back to the dark ages, but I am trying to get you to cover it up. Don't nobody want to see all of that? Take that home and let your husband look at it. If you don't have a husband, you go home and look at it yourself. We don't want to see all that.

Self-Neglect

The virtuous woman does not neglect herself. We need to talk about that because sometimes we as women neglect ourselves. We take care of everybody else and we're sick. We take care of everybody else and we're run down. We take care of everybody else and forget that we have a need. We make sure that Sally has pantyhose, we make sure that you have shoes, we make sure that you ate dinner, and then we forget to get these same things for ourselves. It is not the will of God for us to neglect ourselves. God isn't going to give you any brownie points because you left yourself out. You're not going to get any brownie points for coming to church with a fever. Stay home and take care of that. Your friends and family- love you and want to see you, but if you're sick, they need you to stay home and get well. God isn't going to be mad at you because you were sick. There's no need for you to come to church and bring us all your germs. Then we can't call on the elders of the church because they're all sick! Ask God to help you to stop neglecting yourself.

Sometimes you have to take a mental health day. I take mental health days. I love the sheets and the pillows at the Marriott. I love the sheets and the pillows at the Holiday Inn Express. Every once in a while, I go to visit. I love those covers. Sometimes you have to take a break so that you can hear yourself think. Why? Because you just did all of these things from verse ten all the way to verse twenty-two. You're taking care of everybody else. You're doing all of this stuff for everybody else, but you're forgetting about you. You can't help anybody if you're dead. You can't help anybody if you're sick. You can't help anybody if you're stuck in the hospital somewhere. You've got to learn how to take care of yourself. Put a coat on when you go outside. Cover up your throat with a scarf when it's cold. Learn how to exercise so that you can live longer. Why should we die before our time? These are simple things, but we often neglect ourselves.

What Real Glory Looks Like

Verse twenty-three says, *"Her husband is known in the gates, when he sitteth among the elders of the land."* How is that? That's not from something he did - it's from something she did. From everything she did, she gave him a good name. Isn't it so in society today that when a woman is a mess, they talk about her husband as well? You have to understand that your godly behavior gives a good name to your whole house. Your ungodly behavior gives a bad name to your whole house. If you are a single mother, you aren't exempt - your kids are known by your behavior. The people at the school know that you're crazy and they warn people not to mess with you or your kids. That's just the way it is. We have to be virtuous women who are watchful of our behavior. We need to be women of strength who have good reputations. We need to be women who are good because we have the spirit of God inside of us. We have to make an effort to live holy. We have to make an effort to be good wives, mothers and businesswomen. We have to strive to be good Christians following after God. We can't just come to church just to say we did our "Christian Duty". There is a lifestyle requirement that accompanies our confession of Christianity.

Verses twenty-four and twenty-five tell us that *"She maketh fine linen, and selleth it; and delivereth girdles unto the merchant. Strength and honour are her clothing; and she shall rejoice in time to come."* It may not seem like it's your time to rejoice yet, but your time is coming. You'll be able to rejoice. Sometimes it seems like we are just working and that nothing is happening. It seems that we aren't making any headway nor are we getting any breakthroughs. The scripture says that you are going to rejoice in the time to come. You need to confess with your mouth that you will rejoice in time to come. Your time is coming. You might be crying now, but you won't be crying always. You might not be able to dance right now, but your day is coming in which you will be able to dance until your shoes wear out. Why? Because you're going to wait on God. And waiting on God is NEVER in vain, it ALWAYS pays off!

We learn in verse twenty-six that *"She openeth her mouth with wisdom; and in her tongue is the law of kindness."* This means that she's not talking a lot of dumb stuff. When you start talking, you shouldn't sound like a crazy goof ball. It's a shame. If you don't have anything in your head, then you need to get something in your head. Pick up your Bible and read. In this age of the internet, no one should suffer from ignorance. Even if you can't read, there are audiobooks that will read to you. You are without excuse. A blind man is still able to hear the word of God.

Occupied and Focused

Verse twenty-seven says that *"She looketh well to the ways of her household, and eateth not the bread of idleness."* She's not spending hours doing nothing. The rest of the chapter tells us that *"Her children arise up, and call her blessed; her husband also, and he praiseth her. Many daughters have done virtuously, but thou excellest them all. Favour is deceitful, and beauty is vain: but a woman that feareth the Lord, she shall be praised. Give her of the fruit of her hands; and let her own works praise her in the gates."*

This isn't a competition. It's what goes on in your house that matters. Whatever is going to work in your house, you have to make it work yourself. That isn't anybody else's responsibility. Don't be trying to come up in the church and get your pastor to work out your troubles. Go home and fix it. You might just have to go home and shut up. I have to go home and shut up sometimes. Let somebody else be right sometimes. We don't always have to be right.

If you want to know the secret of being a virtuous woman, you need to walk in the fear of the Lord. The Bible says in Psalm 111:10 that "*The fear of the LORD is the beginning of wisdom.*" This is why we don't have wisdom. We're not walking in the fear of the Lord. Concerning this virtuous woman - on the one hand, her husband's name will be good, and on the other hand, her works will speak for herself. We need to learn how to just get it together. We have to deal with ourselves. We have to learn how to love our neighbors as well as being industrious. We need to be industrious. We need to stop being lazy and making excuses. Get up out of that bed. I know there's just something about that bed that we love, but we need to make ourselves get up out of that bed and get moving. We should strive to be virtuous women. There is no excuse. Obedience to God should be our primary goal. We must be virtuous women. You may not have to sew anybody's clothes or plant vineyards, but you do have a vineyard in the spirit that you can sow into and reap from. You need to make sure that you take care of the vineyard God has allotted to you. God is holding you accountable. You should be able to come before God and lift up holy hands. Don't come in the church living one thing and go out living something else. The person we see you as in the church, at work, or in the grocery story is who we want to see every day. We don't want to relate to you as a stranger, because your behavior makes you unrecognizable. Ask God to make you a virtuous woman in every way. This is His will for you Woman of God.[1]

Section II:

The Secular Historical Viewpoint

"Women are always at the front of revolutions."

~Buthayna Kamel~

As you read the following pages, it is my desire to convey to each reader an understanding the purpose of statistics, sociological studies, and Women's History. This section of this book is meant to reinforce the established contributions of women in the society in which we all live.

There are many struggles endured by the female race that have been outlined and well-documented over the course of time and through the ages. When considering the fact that women have had the tendency to be viewed as an invisible population in the past, it is of utmost importance that within the context of this book, there be provided a reminder and acknowledgment of the facts pertaining to the positive contributions, valiant work and proven history of the power and tenacity of the race known as female end woman.

The tragedies and triumphs of this minority gender and the inclusion of women in our study of history will cause mindsets to be altered and enlightenment to come to any group of individuals that are searching for significance or seeking a positive place in society. The minds of every reader will be challenged, if they have not already, by the startling statistics and historical trends that we have all grown up with, yet somehow never knew it.

Upon reading the pages in this section and the discovery of the amazing heroism, courage and tenacious determination of women in history who fought to come off the fringes of a culture and demanded change so that their voices might be heard will astound many. It is with absolute assurance that the information which preceded this chapter, as well as that which follows, will add to the substantial and extraordinary impact and manner in which women are viewed, addressed and referenced.

9

MEN & WOMEN:

A GLOBAL CONTEXT

"Only dead fish follow the stream."

~Swedish Proverb~

Things are about to get real secular right now. While the spiritual ramifications of the problem women have experienced is of utmost importance, one cannot deny the world-wide effects this prejudice towards women has had on a grander scale. I would like to use a sociological approach to look at the status of women and men globally. A global context is necessary in order to accurately communicate just how pervasive inequality is- in our own backyard and beyond. Many times, we forget that we live in a global society. Though in times past, sharing ideologies beyond our boarders took longer, it was not impossible. Today, with the popularity of internet service, social media and global news agencies, it is easier than ever to proselytize others in other nations to our belief systems and cultures.

That being said, one of the most scathing cultural ills of the west that has been portrayed in all forms globally is sexism. Being of the bel let's get an understanding of what sexism is. It is the belief system of the author, that one cannot live what one does not understand, therefore, we must begin with a working definition of what sexism is. It is the belief that there are innate psychological, behavioral and intellectual differences between men and women; and that these differences connote the superiority of one group and the inferiority of the other. Now in the time in which we live with so much technology and all of the advances in medical science and all of the knowledge that we have access to, why would there still be an issue with sexism? Most believe that the more advanced and progressive a society is, the more one can expect justice and equality. That sounds nice, however, that is most definitely not the case.

As it relates to sexism, we still have much difficulty dealing with its reality. There is yet a large segment of women in global societies who are experiencing sexism in one form or another and they are victims of what in sociology is called double jeopardy. That is when a person is a member of two or more minority groups. In this chapter, we'll look at some of the issues that are pervasive pertaining to sexism as described above. We will also observe how the double jeopardy scenario effects women. women who deal with double jeopardy, number one, they are women, who as a minority group, are also people of color, which is another minority group.

When we look at and focus on gender inequality around the world, it is very notable that

    i.   Over 60,000,000 (sixty million) young girls, (mostly in Asia) are missing and likely they are victims of infanticide, neglect or sex trafficking. Our reality today is that sex trafficking is now an enormous issue; not just in third-world countries, but even here in America.

    ii.   Five hundred thousand women die each year from complications related to childbirth. Mind you, this is a global context. This is not just in America. There are women in other countries who are still suffering and dying because they don't have adequate medical care or medical facilities to birth children.

    iii.   Two thirds of women world-wide are illiterate. Think of the implications of this. Not having the ability to read, write or understand business basics prevent women from earning wages and living above poverty.

iv. One in three women has been abused, beaten, or coerced into sex in an age when we're supposed to be modernized and not barbarian in nature. Women are still being abused, beaten and coerced into sex.

v.   Millions of women have undergone female genital mutilation (FGM), (Clitoridectomy and or infibulation).

Now, those statistics are on the global scale. What about inequality here in the United States?

    ➤ In the U.S., women have lower incomes.
    ➤ They hold fewer prestigious jobs
    ➤ They earn fewer academic degrees
    ➤ They are more likely than men to live in poverty.

You have women who acquired the same degrees as men, have gone to school for the same amount of years, gone through the same training, who then enter into the workforce for the same jobs; These women are still paid less than their male counterparts. Much of this is due to the fact that though we say that we are a modern society, we still have many old-fashioned standards, which apply mostly to the female gender.

Let's take a look at the sociological theories of gender inequality. We will begin with the Structural-Functionalist Perspective. This view gives perspective on the theories of gender and inequality in a pre-industrial society.

❖ Gender based divisions of labor were due to biological necessity of women bearing children, nursing and caring for children; While stronger men provided material needs- and that was functional for society.

❖ In an industrialized society, there were changes in the division of labor and this was due to changes in society such as daycare centers and daycare facilities, lower fertility rates because women were taking birth control and the fact that many jobs did not require physical strength like the preindustrial society.

There is also the Conflict Perspective which states that:

➤ Male dominance and female subordination is due to the relationship men and women have to the production process.

➤ A: In hunting and gathering societies, women and men are equal as each produced needed subsistence.

➤ B: In agricultural and industrial societies, men gained control of production, while women remained in the home to bear and care for children.

➤ C: During World War II, women entered the labor force and now compete with men for jobs.

The last sociological perspective than I would like to deal with, is the Symbolic Interactionist Perspective which declares that:

❖ Gender and gender roles are learned through the socialization process. Meaning we go to school, we see that boys are supposed to play football. Girls are supposed to jump rope, boys play with trucks, girls play with dolls.

❖ Women are socialized into expressive roles, meaning they are nurturers. Women are taught and socialized to be nurturers and are placed into emotionally supportive roles.

Men are socialized into instrumental type roles where they're task oriented versus them being emotional. This perspective shows us how that through socialization and learning from others, whether it be in school or within the home, these are values that are taught; They are not necessarily innate behavioral traits passed on through the creation process. We don't do things simply because one is born a girl. We have been taught to do some of the behaviors we have assumed and now face difficulty dealing inequality because of sexism.

We deal with it within structures and within institutions. (Structural Sexism) This has caused difficulty for women to be able to shatter as it were, "the glass ceiling." It is unfortunate that in 2019, we are still attempting to reach the height of the ceiling to shatter it. In spite of technology and its advances, and the education available, we still have not shattered the proverbial ceiling.

Structural Sexism is the reason why many women earn fewer advanced degrees than men: From childhood women are socialized to choose marriage and motherhood over career and career preparation. Many of you who are reading this today grew up with that very same mentality and it's not necessarily a bad thing. Mind you, I want it to be understood, There is no angry agenda here. I want to present both sides of the spectrum. It is a reality: because of how we have been socialized, this has caused us to choose specific roles- not our innate abilities or ambitions. Many women have become who they are today, because of what society has taught them.

Structural Sexism has caused a gender stratification in our society. We know this and see its effects in the workplace by the fact that the higher the percentage of females there are in an occupation, the lower the pay. This is structural sexism. To clarify exactly what Structural Sexism is; it is the ways in which the organization of society and its institutions subordinate individuals and groups based upon their sex classification.

This leads us to the need to discuss the Devaluation Hypothesis, which argues that women are paid less because the work that they do is socially defined as less valuable than the work performed by men. This is a ludicrous thought. If women do the same job, have the same title and responsibilities, they should get the same pay! I want to remind you that the statistics that I'm sharing with you, are mainly from America, except where noted. America, which is supposed to be the land of opportunity, the home of the free. But as we are learning, is it the norms of American society that have created such an incongruent culture for women.

Work and Structural Sexism

Women make up one third of the world's labor force, although they tend to work in jobs with little prestige, low or no pay, or where no product is produced (service jobs), and then they're also ending up in roles where they are facilitators for others. In other words, they're in a position to facilitate for someone else and get the job done for someone else. In a word, they are a secretary is what that boils down to.

Statistics say "Pink Collar Jobs (low prestige, low wage jobs) are held mostly by women; while "Blue Collar Jobs"(jobs that are not labor oriented), are usually held by the men. More than 70 percent of all minimum wage earners are women. That is a stark and sobering statistic on top of all of the other things that women have to deal with within structural sexism.

Occupational Sex Segregation.

This is when there is a concentration of women in certain occupations and men in other occupations. Sometimes it's inadvertent because of our socialization and how we have been brought up so women will gravitate to certain positions. There are times where women are concentrated in semi-skilled or unskilled occupations, while men are concentrated in professional, administrative and managerial positions. This sex segregation is decreasing because more women are entering into occupations that are dominated by men. They are doing it with difficulty though I might add, but they are entering into these occupations.

Some of the reasons that we are still dealing with Sex Segregation in occupations is:

- Cultural beliefs about what is an appropriate job for a woman or for men. These are still issues. Things like, women shouldn't work on construction… Our government just passed laws recently that allow women to go to combat. That was a debate in Congress because it was not thought that women were built, made or even had the tenacity emotionally to be able to handle war and its evils.

- Through socialization, females and males learn different skills and acquire different aspirations.
- Women have primary responsibility for childcare and choose professions that have flexible hours and career paths. (these are called mommy tracks). Why don't they call them daddy tracks? Because our society is guilty of Occupational Sex Segregation.

Unfortunately, no matter what headway has been made, we are still fighting the same battle. As spoken of before, the "glass ceiling", this invisible barrier that continues to prevent women and other minorities from moving into the top corporate positions, is still a great hindrance to the female gender in the workplace. Who created this ceilng and why is it so difficult to shatter it? We're still waiting for an answer. I know we know what the answer is, but the answer is something that is difficult for us to swallow, and that is that women are still suffering from prejudice. We cannot talk about Structural Sexism without addressing the political structure.

Political Structural Sexism

Do you realize that is still a little less than a hundred years ago that women were given the right to vote when the nineteenth amendment was passed in 1920? Today, women are still less likely than men to be able to hold a political position? Yes, women run for office and many women have been elected, but when running against a male opponent, women are less likely to win. When we look at the election campaign of 2016, with all of the scandals that surrounded both presidential candidates we realize that the female constituent was vilified and criticized in a manner that her male opponent was not. Both had issues that they were dealing with, but when the male counterpart was facing sexism charges and harassment charges, they let him pass. However, if the female candidate had done the same things that he had done, she would have been dropped from the race and considered disqualified. Even as it relates to the press, the big argument used by the media was not pertaining to her political acumen or whether or not she was a qualified candidate, or if she possessed the proper education. Their argument against her was "she's too masculine." "She needs to smile more." These are not the qualities that are going to help her be president. So why were they judging her by these attributes which we're not qualifications for the job? Why was her outward demeaner always the focal point being highlighted by the news? It was not the shining qualifications of the male candidate that won him the election, because he was a Newbie. He had no experience. He's a businessman. Meanwhile, the woman had years of political experience, had already been in the White House as a First Lady, was formerly Secretary of State and was qualified beyond the scope of her opponent. However, it was her gender that lost the race for her and not her character nor her qualifications- or the lack thereof.

Again, I reiterate it is because there is still prejudice against women and Political Structural Sexism is alive and well in the United States of America. Let's let the statistic speak:

- In 2001, women comprised only 10 percent of all governors and held only 13.5 percent of all US congressional seats.
- Worldwide, the percentage of legislative seats held by women ranges from 30 to 40 percent in Scandinavian countries to less than one percent in Middle Eastern and African countries.
- Some countries have quotas to increase women in politics. Countries like India and Brazil are opening the way also Finland, Germany, Mexico, South Africa, and Spain are pushing for the increase of women in politics. That's good news.
- 80 percent of U.S. women believe that by the year 2024, a woman will be in the White House. Well, 2017 could have been that year, however, due to sexism in the political structure that still exists and because it is so pervasive our country, the voters were unable to see beyond the real reason the female candidate was not elected.

Civil Rights, the Law and Structural Sexism.

In 1963, the equal pay act and Title VII of 1964 Civil Rights Act made it illegal for employers to discriminate on the basis of sex; but sex discrimination still occurs. It's illegal, but it is still done-the problem is, it's hard to prove. And now we see with the #METOO Movements' meteoric rise to prominence, sexism in the workplace has now become a big deal and is being addressed by law enforcement as it should have been since Title VII was first ratified into law. Even in Hollywood, the manner in which women have been abused and treated as sex objects for roles, or the way an actress would be considered or denied a role, was based upon the aforementioned. These atrocities were common place, yet, it took years for the law to be enforced. When the women (who were victims) were revealed, it was not acceptable and the men who were the perpetrators were justified by their peers. It was not until everyone got tired and one woman after the other began to stand up against Structural Sexism in Hollywood, that we saw the #METOO rise as a voicein defense of the victims.

Another statistic says that until recently, husbands could rape their wives without fear of persecution or prosecution. And I might add to this, that in 1991 England passed a law that made marital rape a criminal act. In the United States, some states grant a marital-rape exemption, which means that there was no prosecution, provided that the man is living with the woman, married or not. What is going on here? Think about why the prevailing attitude has been that rape cannot take place in marriage or in any other permanent relationship. It makes no sense -just because you're married or in a relationship, that does not give you the right to force sex upon an individual.

 In the U.S., women could enlist in the military but had been given restrictions in their duties. Again, women have only recently been given the greenlight to be allowed to fight in wars. You may need to take a deep breath after reading all of the information that you've just read- and we haven't even dealt with the depths of our culture yet.

Cultural Sexism

American culture has played a major role in influencing sexism and how women are dealt with in society. I want to help you to understand exactly how that is possible. In order to bring clarity, we must understand what Cultural Sexism is. It is the ways in which the culture of society, our norms and values, beliefs and symbols perpetuate subordination based on sex classification.

- ➢ In our culture males and females receive different toys that convey messages about gender. Some of it is correct. Some of it is not.
- ➢ Women work more hours of unpaid labor in the home. (Adult woman work full-time, come home and they work a second shift.) Have you ever thought of it that way- that women get off work and come home to work? That's the second shift.
- ➢ When we go to school, we see how Cultural Sexism is promulgated through our textbooks and other instructional materials, because they perpetuate stereotypes.
- ➢ Males most likely are the ones that participate in the competitive sports. Females are more likely to participate in sports that emphasize individual achievement or cooperation.
- ➢ Teachers are more likely to pay more attention to boys.

Media, Language and Cultural Sexism

It is true when we look at the media, the language that we hear, that Cultural Sexism is a pervasive ill to our society. A study of gender and the images that are found in television, movies, magazines, music, videos, TV commercials, and print media found:

- Media content stresses the importance of appearance and relationships for females; versus the importance of careers and work for males.

- Cultural sexism is reflected in our words and the way that we use them. Our language reflects gender inequality within terms like broad, old maid and spinster. None of which have any male counterpart.

- Placement of sex before titles for specific jobs, e.g., female police officers, male prostitute, things of that nature.

- Male to female differences in communication style reflect the differences in power and socialization. Women seem or at times can be more passive and polite in conversation. Men are less polite, interrupt more often and talk more. And any woman who does the opposite is thought to be un-lady like or rude; however male counterparts may do the same and he's just being a man.

Social Problems and Traditional Gender Role Socialization

We can see in our society that gender roles are changing, but they're changing slowly. In Sociology, this is called "Gender Tourism". This is exemplified by women serving in the military, playing pro basketball, running corporations and governing. They are getting into the political arena, maybe not as frequently or as successfully as men. However, they are entering into the political arena. The affects of Gender Tourism in men is seen when men go on diets, undergo cosmetic surgery, bare their souls in support groups and become cook. There is a need to show balance. I did not want to paint a picture as if all is lost, all is not lost. However, we still have a long way to go. We still have to create for women, in our homes and within every structure and institution- a place within our society that celebrates and honors the value and uniqueness that the female gender brings. It must be agreed upon and implemented that her value is worthy of the same pay, the same honor, and the same respect as her male counterparts.

If we're going to really become a culture that promotes gender equality, we must have a strategy for action. One strategy that some really do not like, especially within the religious community is feminism and the women's movement. Now, before we get into that, you need to do your research because feminism, began as a Christian women's movement. Nowadays, feminism is the belief that women and men should have equal rights and responsibilities, and of course that is the definition I agree with.

The American feminist movement began in 1848, mainly concerned with earning the right to vote for women. These were women who were moved to action because they wanted to be able to let their voice be heard. Also, in our country, we have the National Organization for Women which was established in 1966 and it is the largest feminist organization in the United States. I don't agree with every philosophy of these organizations, however, they do exist, and the purpose is for the equality and quality of life for women.

There's also a men's movement. Some men's organizations advocate gender equality and they oppose feminism and male bashing. I stand against male bashing. I do not agree that in order to bring us to a place of equality that we have to bash our gender counterparts. Some men's groups want equal rights in custody and father's rights; while others for focus on personal growth. It was not until I began my research that I discovered that there was such a thing as a men's movement. I am pleased to know that there are groups advocating for fathers who desire to be active in the lives of their children.

As we close this chapter, we need to address the fact that in the United States, public policy has been created to address the disparities of gender equality. Statutes that have been passed to help reduce gender inequality include the 1963 Equal Pay Act, Title VII of the Civil Rights Act of 1964, Title IX of the Educational Amendment Act of 1972, the Family and Medical Leave Act (FMLA) of 1993, 1994, Violence Against Women Act and the Victims of Trafficking and Violence Protection act of 2000. There have also been Sexual Harassment policies that have been put in force. Title VII of the 1964 Civil Rights Act prohibits sexual harassment involving members of the opposite sex. In 1999, more than 15,000 cases of sexual harassment were reported to the US Equal Employment Opportunity Commission. (There has been a 50 % increase since 1991); Today we have several notable movements that advocate for women experiencing sexual harassment in any form.

To clarify, there are two types of sexual harassment:

> 1. Quid Pro Quo- where an employer requires sexual favors in exchange for promotion, salary increases, other employee benefits.
> The hostile environment that interferes with job performance, which would include things like sexually explicit comments or insults that are made to the employee.

These forms of sexual harassment are prevalent in our culture, government, churches, businesses and organizations. Our country still has a long way to go. We have made very good improvements and progress toward the equality of women, but we are not at the finish line yet.[1]

10

SEXIST EDUCATION

"He asked me, 'What's Your Favorite Position?' I said, 'CEO'!"

~Titular-Journal.com~

One cannot neglect the sociological implications in an educational context related to sexism. First and foremost, we need to understand that education serves as a mechanism for cultural imperialism. Cultural Imperialism simply stated, is just inaccurate indoctrination into the dominant culture of society. We understand that if we want to have our culture of our families impacted, then they must be educated. The dominant culture is taught through the educational system and therefore no matter what you teach your children at home, whenever they go into the school, that cultural imperialism is going to affect their mindsets. It is the norms, the values, the traditions, and the languages of the minorities that are ignored in cultural imperialism. We also find that women being a minority are a part of this subculture who are ignored when looking at statistics worldwide. Over 30 percent of females and 70 percent of males are illiterate when looking at some of the statistics that are available as to how education is available to women and the effect of women not receiving equal education. The contrast or stark worldwide women receive less education than men before the 18 thirties us colleges accepted only male students. Title Eleven of the Education amendments of 1972 states that no person can be discriminated against based on sex in any education program that receives federal funding paragraph designed to end sexism in the hiring, promoting of teachers and administrators in college admissions and financial aid, and then the funding of programs for female athletes. In 1978 point two percent of us women have completed four years of college or more in 2024 percent had completed four years of college. More females tend to lag behind males in math and science. And so these are some of the contrast with the statistics on succeeds and these things are a result of inequality in education. And we cannot think about how gender roles and sexism is affecting women without thinking about and analyzing how education plays a big part in that. The more we know, the more we're able to do and the more that we have access to knowledge and the ability to further educations as women, it makes better jobs, more accessible health care, and being able to provide for families, especially if you are a single woman.

These issues are urgent, and it all begins with education. It is said that education, you know, as related to the structural functional perspective, it serves as an important task for society such as instruction, socialization, sorting individuals into various statuses and custodial care, and this is where we need to be able to address sexism and education for the simple fact that we are still classifying people in hierarchies of people, groups, the educated and the uneducated.[1]

11

HIS-STORY:

WOMEN THROUGH THE AGES

"Single: (noun), A man who makes jokes about women in the kitchen."

~Someone Who Got Jokes~

There is something to be said for an accurate historical account. Although many would like to disregard what is known about the past, it is of utmost urgency that we not repeat many of the mistakes documented from the past. We cannot call ourselves a "progressive society" and continue to maintain antiquated practices as it pertains to the treatment, education and liberation of women.

The following historical information may be found with a simple click of the mouse. The issue isn't that the information is locked up in a vault somewhere. The issue is that we as a society refuse to banish barbaric thoughts and practices as it relates to women. Although a great deal of the prejudice and mistreatment of the female gender may not be blatant or overt, it still does exist. It is not until those who have been placed in authority, namely men, take a stand and refuse to repeat a negative history by doing to women today what historians have clearly and accurately documented as abuse, prejudice and hate towards a demographic in society who has created change and contributed to the growth and positive change of nations the world over.

Allow History to educate you and speak for the women whose voices in times past were forced into silence.

<u>**Aegean Connections**</u>

A. There were many similarities between the Minoan Crete and Mycenean Greece Civilizations.

1. Minoan Civilization spanned from 3100-1000 B.C.E. and was the called the most successful Bronze Age Civilization due to their advances in fine art, architecture, and thriving economy. The cities of the civilization included Knossos, Mallia, Phaistos, and Ayia Triadha and were known for their magnificent palaces. This is significant because their economy was centered around the working in or for the palace. The palace workers were responsible for goods such as textiles which were distributed at home as well as traded with those of foreign lands. There was the use of flax by spinners and weavers who used sheep's wool to make dyed cloths that were prized by far- away lands.

2. Mycenaen Civilization spanned from 1650-1100 BCE. This civilization reached its height from 1400-1250 BCE. It was from this place and during this time that scholars believed the customs and beliefs in the classical Greek gods, and myths evolved. The Mycenaens were a literate people who used an early form of Greek called Linear B. This people also had palaces as the central focus of their lives as well as the worship of their gods. Linear B tablets listed the names of thirty gods and goddesses, who were considered Greek deities. To name a few, they were, Hera, Zeus, and Poseidon. These gods owned property and slaves. Some women served as Priestesses, in what was considered a prominent position as well as Keybearers who were in charge of controlling the sacred treasure which was at the cult site where worship took place.

B. Early Greek Civilization 750-500 B.C.E.

1. During this period, the Phoenician alphabet was the basis in writing as it re-emerged and iron began to replace bronze as the metal of choice. Trade of wine, olive oil other goods of the Mediterranean became popular again. This was known as the Archaic Period and lasted until the fifth century B.C.E. This period suffered from a scarcity of sources and as a result, the women are not easily differentiated from this and the Classical Period. Since there are no reliable points of reference to identify women of the Archaic Period, myths served as a point of reference to describe the details of the roles of women and gender expectations.

2. Greek Poetry and Myths portrayed women of the Archaic Period with the expectations, traditions, and mindsets of Greek society. The earliest writings are the epic poems by Hesiod and Homer which showed women in both positive and negative light, based upon the writer's own outlook of women at the time of their writings. Women were portrayed as either priestesses,

goddesses, or as the Amazonian women who in myth were warriors who didn't need men for companionship or reproduction. I believe this was showing that there was a bit of a rebellion brewing among the women and the poets wanted to let it be known that they were aware of the displeasure of the women in their roles at the time.

<u>Sex and Sexuality in Classical Greece 7th Century B.C.E.</u>

Greek Masculinity and Homosexuality

1. Masculinity:

 High value was placed on masculinity in the Greek culture and this gave way for women to be subordinate to men. Men had to prove their masculinity in three ways: As head of household, he proved his character by showing he could control his house, children and wives. As a soldier he proved he was fearless and possessed strength, and finally as a gymnast- he had to show he could stand up to the rigors of intense physical activity, thereby gaining him a place of honor in society.

2. Homosexuality

. Homosexual relationships were typical displays of strength and veracity as older men engaged in sex acts with younger men who participated under the strict constraints of the social hierarchy. The same dominance that was exercised by males over females was likewise employed in the male-to-male relationships. It was a show of strength to have one man dominate and show strength over a weaker, younger male.

Sex Gender and Greek Philosophy C.A. 540 B.C.E.

1. Differences between men and women made for interesting ideologies during this period of time. Democritus (460-370 B.C.E.) was the first to differentiate the woman from the man and to claim the woman was inferior to man and that man was superior. There were medical teachings by Hippocrates that supposedly proved that men and women were different and that men and women could determine the gender of their children based

upon their secretions, and balancing Humors from the body. Women were thought to need t remain pregnant, lactating or on their menses in order to remain healthy. No such rules were regulated for men.

2. It was thought that women, like animals needed the supervision of a man in order to function in society properly. Greek philosophers looked to the spiritual world for proofs of their theories of women's inferiority. These expectations would stick to societies for centuries to come.

Changes Come to the Mediterranean: Societies decline and open opportunities for women. Athens was one of those places that when they were in decline, doors opened up for women to walk in equality in the city. Women were able to take their place in politics in the court of Phillip of Macedon. Alexander's conquests brought the opportunity for women to become part of powerful dynasties and to extend the culture of the Greeks to other places. The intermingling of the Greeks and non-Greeks allowed new ideas to be exchanged and doors of opportunity to be open to all of the women dwelling in the Mediterranean region.

The expectations on gender have evolved from the period of the Bronze Age cultures of the Aegean Sea. Women at one point were thought of in terms of their utility in marriage alliances and were kept marginalized from society and political life. As times changed, Hellenistic women were included in economics, politics, and culture which showed a stark contrast of times before and these changes had a huge impact upon society and were responsible for contributing many positive things to their world.

I: Women and Judaism In the First Century

A. This chapter begins with the many life experiences of the Jewish

women. Many became members of various groups which

encouraged celibacy and abstaining from worldly pleasures.

1.   Many women obtained important positions of authority in

the synagogues, but in the city of Jerusalem women were

stilled banned from going into any part of the temple except one portion.

2.   A group of writings gathered after the Romans defeated and captured Jerusalem in 70 CE, the *Talmud* idealized the restrictions on women in place across the Jewish community, banning them from possessing an independent, legal, or religious identity.

II. Female Followers of Jesus

A.   Paul laid the groundwork for ideologies concerning Christian women.

1.   Writings of early Christianity, to include Paul's letters, the Gospels and the Gnostic Gospels, show the impact and importance of women during the times of Christ and even while presenting untrue and misinformation about the nature of women and appropriate place.

2.   The above-mentioned texts speak of Jesus' discontent with the traditional Graeco-Roman family by the preaching and encouraging of celibacy. In addition to presenting women as equals (in the spiritual sense), the Gnostic Gospels acknowledged and made reference to women being apostles

and presented a complex theology on gender in which God was both male and female.

III. Living and Thinking as a Christian

A. The Christians set themselves apart due to their proselytizing of others.

1. Opportunities in the early church were available for women to live beyond gender expectations and they were martyrs, deacons and patrons just as some men were.

2. It seems as pressure mounted, and the activities of women were on the rise, and the church followed the path of becoming more institutionalized, it prevented women from a vast array of the fundamental activities, limited to preaching and baptism, all the while, pressuring them with the impossible ideal of embracing motherhood, while remaining celibate as the Virgin Mary.

IV. Living Like a Man: The Christian Ascetic Ideal

A. Christian women could express their Faith through monasticism and asceticism which allowed them to have liberties that were unavailable to Pagan women.

1.   Early Christian women and men rejected marriage, family
     and worldly goods in a pursuit of spirituality, retreating
     initially into the desert and then into monastic communities.

2.   Early church fathers Jerome and Augustine amplified the
     difficulties for holy women who had to overcome their flaws
     but could not agree on the ideas concerning marriage and
     sexuality. The idea of traditional family life was rejected,
     paving the way for many women to override gender issues
     and obtain authority within Christianity.

V. Women and the Rise of Byzantium

Another gender category in Constantinople, were Eunichs, which had qualities that were usually attributed to one or the other sex. Some eunuchs, just like empresses, held great authority because of palace associations. The women of Byzantium were expected to submit to Roman law as well as to the traditions of the Greeks; while women had the right to own property, like other societies, women of lower social classes suffered from fewer restrictions and held a several different types of positions as workers. Just as the west, living in convents provided women the chance to exercise in ministry in the areas of patronage and spirituality.

<u>Gender in Germanic Society</u>

A. The Germans were many tribes living east of the Danube and Rhine Rivers.
1. Much of the norms about Germanic gender came from Cornelius Tacitus a Roman Senator.
2. They believed that women were prophetic, had an element of holiness, and should be regarded.
B. Germanic Legal Codes and the Restructuring of Society
1. These codes established monetary values, or Wergelds, for all members of society.
2. Women's Wergelds depended upon her social status and childbearing ability

Carolingian Transformations

A. The most successful Germanic kingdom developed in the eighth century under Charlemagne and his heirs.
1. Charlemagne built his capital at Aachen as the new Byzantium and intervened in religious debates.
2. The Pope was persuaded by Charlemagne's logic and made him emperor.
B. Carolingian Marriage Reform
1. Charlemagne and Louis the Pious pressed for Christian ideals in marriage, its sanctity, and permanence.
2. Wives gained status within the family because they were no longer disposable.

Women on the Frontlines: The Second Wave of Invasions

A. Women suffered horrific violence but also were key participants in the settlement and integration of the new peoples who came from other lands.
1. Most women tended farms, raised children, and sewed, while others went on raiding expeditions, and engaged in trade.
2. Intermarriage between the Vikings and Anglo-Saxon women became more prevalent in English settlements.
B. Invaders in Eastern Europe
1. Invaders disrupted political, religious, and economic life in Eastern Europe. Several assaults were made on Constantinople and it was nearly conquered.
2. The interaction of pagan and Christian cultures redefined women's honor. Some rituals included abduction games which took place marriage rites.

Medieval Social Organization
A. A military elite was created by the repeated invasions. These soldiers lived off the labor of the population that was dependent upon them.

1. Society was broken up into three orders: those who fight, those who pray, and those who work.

2. Men and women from the three orders were fleeing to new and revitalized cities in search of life outside the military concerns of the countryside.

B. Aristocratic Women

1. The aristocrats made up less than 5 percent of the population. These people formed the basis of medieval gender norms.

2. Noblewomen attempted to limit men's violence with creation of a court culture known as chivalry which guided the norms of the society of that time.

Women and Church Reform

A. Women were seen as having too much freedom due to the invasions and the church sought to bring things back under control.

1. Women attempted to recreate the Cluniac Ideals and it was frowned upon by the men. Cluny did not create a house for women until 1055.

2. The Cistercian Order was another popular order that was created to counter the Cluniac Orders and its ideals.

B. The Cistercian Order remained popular among women who longed for apostolic poverty and personal relationship with God appealing.

1. Robert D'Arbrissell understood the power of female spirituality and worked to cultivate it. He set out to maintain a new style of religious life for women.

2. D'Arbristrell founded the Order of Fontervault which expanded and attracted many followers. He limited contact between men and women and divided the community work between them.

Gregorian Reforms and the New Gender Order

A. The Cluniac reforms set the stage for the Gregorian reforms. This was the first European-wide attempt at ecclesiastical change and reorganization.

1. By the 9th and 10th century, the papacy had lost most of its international influence and had fallen under the control of a few Roman families.

2. Observers of the aristocratic interventions were harshly criticized the influence of women on the pope. Calls for reform began with a smear campaign.

B. Politics portrayed women as debauchers and manly and defined politics as a purely masculine activity.

1. Cardinals initiated a series of reforms designed to liberate the papacy from Roman politics, strengthen ecclesiastical organization, and improve clerical morality.

2. Ending nepotism and simony theoretically gave the church more control over who became clerics and what offices they filled, removing the church and familial relationships.

Female Monastic Culture During the High Middle Ages

A. The Convent remained central to many women although the church refused to involve women in monastic reform.

1. Life in the convent was attractive to women because it seemed full of the promise of salvation for them.

2. During the 12th and 13th centuries, convents were the producers of many dynamic women who where great thinkers and artists. Convents became the place where women's culture flourished.

B. Women could not perform mass or administer sacraments.

1. Although they were restricted, women found other ways to show their talents and participate in the liturgy.

2. Nuns created great important works of art, literary works that assisted in relaying information to assist women as they lived and experienced life in the convent.

Conclusion

A. Female religious life present many paradoxes for women.

1. Women had many opportunities to serve God and feel part of religious life as well as experiencing many constraints placed upon them which inhibited their abilities to serve in the manner of male priests.

2. Heloise and Aberlard married and their relationship suffered as a result of the paradoxes of convent life. They were apart for nearly a decade and despite this separation, she maintained passion for him and became distraught about her monastic lifestyle.

B. The religious reforms of the High Middle Ages altered the gender norms of that era.

1. The reforms institutionalized the beliefs in women's inherent weakness and sinfulness. The Cluniac reforms devalued nun's contributions to monastic life.

2. Women's opportunities expanded with the waves of chaos and political stability of repeated invasions.

3. Kings who reasserted their control, caused restrictions on the liberties of women.

4. Political stability ensured greater safety for women, but usually their ability to get out and do more was inhibited as a result.

This is but a snapshot of the history of the treatment and advancement of women. As time progressed, it is noted that women have been given greater responsibility and freedom within the religious community. One fact is undeniable however, women have shown their strength and worth at every turn in the various religious movements referenced above.

It is my prayer that history not continue to repeat itself by giving a semblance of liberty to women while never truly releasing her to fulfil her divine assignments along-side her male counterparts; with whom she's truly a co-laborer and comrade in arms!

Works Cited

Katherine L. French, Allyson M. Poska. *Women & Gender In the Western Past , Volume 1: To 1815*. Boston: Houghton Mifflin Company, 2007. Book.

EPILOGUE

"Barring women from ministry is heresy; and those who teach such

will have to answer to God for it."

~Dave Ward~

The Case for Women as Apostles, Bishops, Overseers,

Pastors, & Elders.

The purpose of this chapter is for closing remarks and to draw the final conclusion on this matter. The truth is, once you read the following reference information, you will see that for ions, Scripture as literally been taken out of context and many have used a play on words to confuse and divert others from the truth.

It is a fact as proven through the previous chapters and the reference materials following the Bible DOES affirm and allow women to be Pastors, bishops, Overseers and Apostles. It has been the influence of a patriarchal society and church that has prohibited the will of God- against what has been taught through Scripture. We may therefore conclude that any teaching/doctrine that denies, prohibits or otherwise hinders qualified women from assuming the positions of authority and leadership as described in the Bible should henceforth be deemed heretical and erroneous. This teaching must be exposed, rejected and dismissed and no longer embraced or disseminated by or through the Ecclessia. We are in need of audacious leaders who will stand for truth and have an unwavering spirit as years of false doctrine is torn from the annals of time and rejected by a Church who desires nothing but unadulterated TRUTH- even if it kills our sacred cows of patriarchy, sexism and misogyny!

Study the notes below well. Go back and read the previous chapters and as you do, challenge yourself to ask the difficult questions. Are you willing to relearn what you thought you already knew? Can you accept that you may have had it wrong from the beginning? Will you be able to release into leadership other women who have incorrectly been muted, marginalized and otherwise ousted from position, because of erroneous teaching that are rooted in upholding one gender in preference above another- all due to misinterpretation of The Word of God?

One last note about Apostleship, what has not been specifically addressed by title in the text of this book, still applies. If women, according to Scripture may hold all other titled positions, that Office of Apostle is no different. This applies to all of the Five-Fold Offices as mentioned in Ephesians 4:11; Acts 15:4 and the fact that the word used in 1 Timothy 5:1 Presbuturos when clearly defined omits gender and one is solely chosen on the merit of life experience. But for those who take issue with gender and deeper study of this word is clearly defined in the Greek as an older woman. I believe that indeed settles the score.

Elder Defined

A name frequently used in the Old Testament as denoting a person clothed with authority, and entitled to respect and reverence (Genesis 50:7). It also denoted a political office (Numbers 22:7). The "elders of Israel" held a rank among the people indicative of authority. Moses opened his commission to them (Exodus 3:16).

The "elders" of the New Testament church were the "pastors" (Ephesians 4:11), "bishops or overseers" (Acts 20:28), "leaders" and "rulers" (Hebrews 13:7 ; 1 Thessalonians 5:12) of the flock. Everywhere in the New Testament bishop and presbyter are titles given to one and the same officer of the Christian church. He who is called presbyter or elder on account of his age or gravity is also called bishop or overseer with reference to the duty that lay upon him (Titus 1:5-7 ; Acts 20:17-28 ; Phil 1:1; 1 Tim. 5:1).

New Testament elders (presbyteroi [presbuvtero"]) are also called bishops (episkopoi [ejpivskopo"]) without implying any essential difference in the office referred to. In Acts 20:17, 28 and tit 1:5, 7 the two names are used interchangeably. Also the requirements for the office of the elders and bishops are very similar (cf. Titus 1:5-9 ; and 1 Tim 3:1-7). The term "elder" stresses the connection with the age of the office bearer, while the term "bishop" emphasizes the nature of the task that is to be done. A distinction is made (in 1 Tim 5:17) between those elders who rule well, especially those who labor in the preaching and teaching (who are now called ministers), and others (who are now referred to as elders and whose full-time task is directing the affairs of the church).

With respect to the duties of an elder, there is a continuity with the basic tasks of the elder in the Old Testament. All elders have the task of oversight and discipline of the congregation (Acts 20:28) and all have the responsibility to rule and guide the people of God with the Word in a manner that is pleasing to God (Acts 20:29-31). Also elders in the new dispensation are to preserve and nurture life with God in the covenant community (1 Thess 2:11-12). In executing this task they are in the service of their risen Lord (to whom they will have to give account 1 Thess 5:12 ; Heb 13:17) and they are empowered by his Spirit (Acts 20:28 ; 1 Col 12:4-6[1]

Bishop Defined

This is a study of the word bishop as it appears in 1 Timothy 3: 1, 2. In the various versions, other words are substituted for bishop. The whole chapter deals with the qualifications of bishops and deacons in the New Testament church. Only the first two qualifications are included in this study as the primary

interest here is the use of the word 'bishop' and its substitutes.
The renderings of twenty-three versions are listed here. Other
versions use these terms and the wording of the qualifications.
Explanations from other versions and four other reference
books may alsobe found and studied. It is recommended to also
peruse commentary on what has been written.[2]

NBV – Footnote: "Bishop" is translated from the Greek
episkopos, meaning literally overseer. In the first century
episkopos, bishop or overseer, and presbuteros, elder, were used
interchangeably, eg. Titus 1: 5 and 7, where both words refer to
the same office. After the first century the office of bishop or
overseer over that of elder developed.[3]

Vine's Complete Expository Dictionary of

Old and New Testament Words:

Episkopos, lit. an overseer, whence English "bishop,"
which has precisely the same meaning, is found in Acts 20: 28;
Philippians 1: 1; 1 Timothy 3: 2; Titus 1: 7; 1 Peter 2: 25. Note:
Presbuteros, "an elder," is another term for the same person as
bishop or overseer. See Acts 20: 17 with verse 28. The term
"elder" indicates the mature spiritual experience and
understanding of those so described; the term "bishop," or
"overseer," indicates the character of the work undertaken.
According to the divine will and appointment, as in the NT,
there were to be "bishops" in every local church, Acts 14: 23;
Acts 20: 17; Philippians 1: 1; Titus 1: 5; James 5: 14.[4]

BREAK THAT DOWN AGAIN PLEASE?

I would like to take another look at the words, Overseer, Bishop, Pastor
and Elder, breaking down the same words as above, yet using a different
resource to solidify the accuracy of the points stated above. At the risk of
being redundant, it is my hope that the following entries will provide a
self-explanatory assessment of the words above as it pertains to women in
leadership and authority in the Church. If there is one thing that is

abundantly clear, it is the fact that there have been many prejudices as it relates to the understanding and release of women in authority. It is without question as one reads the definitions/translations of the Greek words given, that those who have taught the Scriptures, blatantly disregard the truth presented right before them. Though they decipher the words accurately, the constant use of the male gender as the "rule" is referenced even when the same words are used in a feminine sense having the exact same meaning as the male reference. It is therefore the opinion of the author that this is a tragic disregard for TRUTH to reinforce the heresy of Patriarchy and to keep the female gender from occupying seats of authority within the church.

Titus 2:3

πρεσβυς

The noun πρεσβυς (presbus) means "first-comer" or "foregoer". It does not refer to some kid who's been elected "elder" by a band of nitwits. It also does nor refer to someone who needs to wear some symbol or tag to be identified as one. Our word refers to someone of middle age, someone old enough to have adult children, who's been around the block and who has experienced and survived most common challenges life may throw at a person. Highly intelligent animals such as elephants naturally follow their most experienced matriarchs, and so-called orphan herds (groups that have lost their experienced elders) often succumb or else survive at the lowest rungs of the pecking order. Less intelligent animals put their most experienced elders in homes and follow leaders with the best TV commercials.

Our word πρεσβυς (presbus) stems from the familiar Proto-Indo-European root per-, meaning first, that also gave us pro-words such as "professor," pre-words like "premier," and words that have to do with leadership such as "priest" and primality such as "prime." Some scholars believe that our word has two parts and that the second part comes from the PIE root gwa-, meaning to go or come. This would make a presbus literally a man who's gone before or a man who came earlier.

In the classics our noun often emphasizes a literal great age but certainly implies wisdom, pre-eminence and leadership. In some societies (like Sparta) our word presbus or "First Comer" was used as a political title meaning president, or someone presiding (same word) over a ruling council. By the time the New Testament was written this once very common word appears to have gone out of use.

In the New Testament only the following derivations occur: The verb πρεσβευω (presbeuo) meaning to be a foregoer. In the classics this verb may refer to age (to be the "first-comer/elder" of two brothers) but by the time of the New Testament this verb referred to the function and status of "one who goes before," which in turn either denoted a leader or an ambassador. Ambassadors were people who were sent by their lords into foreign territories, to establish a base there and to prepare a proper climate for their lord to be received in. Our verb is used in 2 CORINTHIANS 5:20 and EPHESIANS 6:20 only, but obviously in the latter sense of being ambassadors, in the words of Isaiah, "clearing the way for the Lord in the wilderness, and making smooth in the desert a highway for our God" (Isaiah 40:3).

From this verb in turn comes: The noun πρεσβεια (presbeia), a going before. This noun literally describes the act of the verb: the fact or length of the foregoing (that is: age or seniority). Drawn from the more modern use of New Testament times, this noun describes the nature, office and business of ambassadors: embassage or embassy (LUKE 14:32 and 19:14 only). The latter Lucan story rather obviously hints at Herod's flight to Rome in 40 BC, where he was crowned King of the Jews and received funding to return and actually conquer Jerusalem. He did so and murdered everyone who got in his way, including the last of the Hasmoneans — who happened to also include his wife and sons; a brutality revisited in the story of the slaughter of the children of Bethlehem (MATTHEW 2:16).

The adjective πρεσβυτερος (presbuteros), which describes a pertaining to first-coming or foregoing, which in turn either means being old (being first-coming in time; LUKE 15:25), being pre-pre-eminent (having rank or status in society) or else being an ambassador (preparing things for the arrival of the sending lord). The ancients appear to have viewed older people as ambassadors "sent back in time" by future generations, to prepare the world for the arrival of these future generations (Psalm 102:18).

The gospel of Jesus Christ has not a lick to do with some religion and everything with the Logos, or natural law upon which all things operate (COLOSSIANS 1:16-17, ROMANS 1:20). An intimate understanding of natural law leads to science and technology but also to social justice and responsibility and proper stewardship. Ultimately, when a conscious understanding of natural law governs humanity (REVELATION 21:22-23), humanity will live in utter freedom in a perfect society (JOHN 8:32).

Up until today the first line of ambassadors of Jesus the Logos consist of folks who urge others to respect the facts rather than suspicions, logic rather than fear, and diplomatic convention rather than domination and dominion. Ambassadors of Christ have always been rare (most people are by nature ambassadors of the other guy) but the last decade or so the numbers have rapidly increased. Our adjective is used 67 times, often substantially; SEE FULL CONCORDANCE.

From it in turn come:The noun πρεσβυτεριον (presbuterion), which describes the place, gathering or agency of presbuteroi, whether these presbuteroi are old guys, political leaders or ambassadors. In practice this word describes the office and acts of a council of leaders. It occurs in LUKE 22:66, ACTS 22:5 and 1 TIMOTHY 4:14 only.

The comparative noun πρεσβυτης (presebutes), literally meaning an "earlier-comer". It denotes a man who is older than someone who could be expected to lead a community on account of his great experience; a generation older than a πρεσβυς (presbus). Our word usually denotes a geriatric man (LUKE 1:18, TITUS 2:2) but in PHILEMON 1:9 it applies to Paul, who was a νεανιας (neanias), or "young man" at the stoning of Stephen (ACTS 7:58), at best thirty years earlier.

This suggests that the author of Philemon may have regarded Paul as the earlier foregoer or trailblazing ambassador. Our word occurs only these three times.

The noun πρεσβυτις (presbutis), which is not really a wholly separate word but rather the feminine version of the previous one. It denotes an elderly woman (TITUS 2:3 only). Together with the preposition συν (sun), meaning together or with: the noun συμπρεσβυτερος (sumpresbuteros), meaning fellow foregoer (1 PETER 5:1 only). This word appears to reflect a relatively common term in the Greco-Roman world, namely that of fellow-ambassador or one's colleague at an embassy[5]

"All logic should be consistent and applied across the board. The order of Creation is as follows: plants, fish, animals, man, woman. One of the first commands in Scripture is for woman to lead!" (Gen 1:27)

Dave Ward

Commendations

Apostle Francesca Stubbs has written a thoughtful, insightful book that will challenge traditional paradigms. Apostle Stubbs powerfully, but gently challenges the reader to go deeper than they've gone before. This book is provocative and thought provoking. A MUST READ!!

Overseer Kevin K. Penceal, Sr.

Triumph Church of Christ, Mt. Vernon, NY

Real Talk, "Woman Shut Your Mouth" is very challenging, impressive and thought-provoking! I was born and raised in a church with strict guidelines for women; particularly those who acknowledged and expressed their call to preach the Gospel of Jesus Christ. My attitude was malicious and unresponsive to women who preached, taught a Sunday School class, and I walked out whenever a woman got up to speak. Today, I can honestly say, God has delivered me from nearly 20 years of immature thinking and feelings towards women who lead. Women, I encourage you to speak up and speak loud!

Pastor Stephen Hilton

Rehoboth Church, Atlantic City, NJ

The evidence of the Scriptures and revelation that

has been revealed through this book will definitely open up many eyes and ears to what has been falsified by man for many years. (I believe) women are were not just (created) to be seen, but heard as well.

Apostle Nichole S. Echols

Rebirth Worship Ctr. Chicago, Illinois

For me, this was not just a good read, as many books or sections of books are classified. This is life changing. I felt the chapter on Submission was though-provoking, insightful and methodical. The author's perspective is unbiased and will transform old mindsets and beliefs in a scholarly fashion. Her research Is substantial, relevant, excellent and unquestionably proven.

Those who are privileged to read this published work, in particular the chapter on Submission, will have all preconceived perceptions about "submission" pertaining to women within our society, systematically dispelled.

Pastor Norma Wilson Neal

N.D.N. Administrative Services, Fayetteville, NC

Contributors

Dr. Susan Stubbs-Hyatt, Church historian, Bible scholar, ordained minister and life-long professional educator. She is also the co-founder of Hyatt Int'l. Ministries and Hyatt Press, as well as the Int'l Christian Women's Hall of Fame, located in Grapevine, TX., where she resides with her husband Dr. Eddie L. Hyatt. Dr. Stubbs-Hyatt is also the author of several books.

Margaret Mowczko, is a teacher of religious education, the piano and a blog writer. She manages her online groups; Every Old Testament Woman, and God's Word to Women. Marg is an experienced Singer, songwriter and is an advocate for gender equality and Christian egalitarianism. She has written countless articles on the subject which has transformed the lives of her readers.

Marg is a native of Sydney Australia where she resides with her Husband Pete, along with her children and grandchildren.

Bibliography

Chapter 1:

1. Me Obey Him; Handford, Elizabeth Rice; Sword of the Lord Publishers; 1972; 31; revised edition, 1994; Murphreesboro, Tn
2. Me Obey Him; Handford, Elizabeth Rice; Sword of the Lord Publishers; 1972; 35; revised edition, 1994; Murphreesboro, Tn
3. Me Obey Him; Handford, Elizabeth Rice; Sword of the Lord Publishers; 1972; 35; revised edition, 1994; Murphreesboro, Tn
4. 1 Corinthians 12:7; English Standard Version

Chapter 3:

1. In the Beginning; 129; Facing the Consequence
2. Liddell-Scott-Jones Lexicon; 1843; Oxford Clarendon Press
3. John 16:13; English Standard Version
4. Marg Mowczko; Teshuqah; Equality and Gender in Genesis 1-3; November 7, 2015

Chapter 4:

1. In the Spirit We're Equal, The Sprit, The Bible and Women: A Revival Perspective; Chapter 16; 245-246; Hyatt International Ministries; 1998; Stubbs-Hyatt, Susan
2. In the Spirit We're Equal, The Sprit, The Bible and Women: A Revival Perspective; Chapter 16; 247-249; Hyatt International Ministries, Int'l.; 1998; Stubbs-Hyatt, Susan
3. The Merriam-Webster's Dictionary; new edition, 2016
4. The Spirit, The Bible and Women; Teaching and Study Guide; 141-142; 1999; Hyatt International Ministries; Stubbs-Hyatt, Susan
5. In the Spirit We're Equal, The Sprit, The Bible and Women: A Revival Perspective; Chapter 16; 257-258; Hyatt International Ministries; 1998; Stubbs-Hyatt, Susan

Chapter 5

1. Veiled and Silenced: How Culture Shaped Sexist Theology;1989;139; Schmidt, Alvin. J

2. Veiled and Silenced: How Culture Shaped Sexist Theology;1989;139-140; Schmidt, Alvin J.

3. Daily Life in Rome; E.O .Lorimer; Carcopino, Jerome; New Haven; Yale University Press; 1940; 95

4. In Livy's From the Founding City, Volume #9; Cambridge; Harvard University Press, 1936; 416

5. Veiled and Silenced: How Culture Shaped Sexist Theology;1989;146; Schmidt, Alvin. J.

6. Veiled and Silenced: How Culture Shaped Sexist Theology;1989;149; Schmidt, Alvin. J

7. Veiled and Silenced: How Culture Shaped Sexist Theology;1989;154-155; Schmidt, Alvin. J

8. Attitude Lutherans Should Take Towards Women's Suffrage; Sieck, Louis; Lutheran Witness; 38:13; May 1919; 180

9. Shall Women Vote?: MCKee, John V.; Catholic World; 102; October 1915; 52

10. New Woman, New Earth; Cited by Ruether, Rosemary; Seabury Press; New York; 1975; 22

11. Veiled and Silenced: How Culture Shaped Sexist Theology;1989;161; Schmidt, Alvin. J

12. Patterns of Authority in the Early Church; Scholer, David; 1993; 43

13. 10 Things Jesus Taught About Women, And A Few Things He Didn't Teach; Stubbs-Hyatt, Susan;2009; Hyatt Press; 11

Chapter 6

1. Girl Get a Grip: Business and Coaching Edition; Shattering Perceptions; Stubbs, Francesca; Sodaan Publishing; 2016

Chapter 7

1. Token Girl, Token Female; Pollit, Katha; TvTropes.org; 1991

2. The Smurfette Principle; Pollit, Katha, 1991

3. T.V. Tropes; The Smurfs; 1991

4. Never A Self-Made Woman; 1991

Chapter 8

1. Girl Get a Grip: Business and Coaching Edition; Virtue, Women and Reality T.V.; Stubbs, Francesca; Sodaan Publishing; 2016

Chapter 9

1. Understanding Social Problems, 5th Edition; Mooney, Knox & Schacht; Thompson, Wadsworth; 2006.

Chapter 10

1. Understanding Social Problems, 5th Edition; Mooney, Knox & Schacht; Thompson, Wadsworth; 2006.

Chapter 11

1. Women and Gender in Western Past, Volume One to 1815; French, Poska;

Epilogue

1. Easton's Illustrated Dictionary of the Bible, 3rd Edition; Public Domain; Thomas Nelson Publishers; 1897 (Elder).
2. Easton's Illustrated Dictionary of the Bible, 3rd Edition; Public Domain; Thomas Nelson Publishers; 1897 (Bishop).
3. The Tyndale Archive; NBV Footnote; Zondervan; 1969;
4. Vine's Complete Dictionary of O,T. and N.T.Words; Vine, W.E.; AMG Publishers; 1998

Other Works By the Author

The Battle of the Overcomer: A Spiritual Warfare Guide for the Believer

ISBN-13: 978-1469904160

ISBN-10:1469904160

BISAC: Religion/Christian Life/Spiritual Warfare

Girl Get A Grip: A Woman's Guide to Surviving Adversity (Handbook)

ISBN-13: 978-1499686234

ISBN-10: 1499686234

BISAC: Religion/Christian Ministry/General

***Girl Get A Grip: A Woman's Guide to Surviving Adversity* (Workbook)**

ISBN-13: 978-1512164077

ISBN-10: 1512164077

BISAC: Religion/Christian Ministry/General

Girl Get A Grip: Business and Coaching Edition

ISBN-13: 9781976551772

ISBN-10: 1976551773

BISAC: Women/Business

About the Author

Francesca Stubbs is a global speaker who has ministered on platforms in the U.S. and overseas. She is an Apostle and most recently has been appointed Bishop Designate in the Lord's church. She is also a successful Entrepreneur. Her business acumen has allowed her the privilege to work in various sectors of the business world, providing mentoring, corporate counseling/coaching, as well as working with individuals to create nonprofit enterprises and education hubs.

She has appeared on several International Christian Television programs to share her testimony, talk about her books and to preach the Word of God. She currently travels the world providing ministry training, Increase Now Financial seminars for ministries and businesses as well as ministering the Gospel of Jesus Christ.

Francesca has been married to her highschool sweetheart, Javer for 30 years together, they are the proud parents of four (4) adult children: Jessica, Ijason, Javer Jr., and Francesca Darnelle

Speaking Ministry

Contact Info:

SODAAN GLOBAL

P.O. Box 229

Spring Lake, NC 28390

Office Phone: (910) 239-7923 or (910) 321-5964

Email: sodaanmedia@gmail.com

Website: www.sodaanglobal.org

Connect with the Author on Social Media:

Facebook: www.facebook.com/apostlefran2014

www.facebook.com/SODAANGLOBAL

Twitter: www.twitter.com/ApostleFran

Instagram: @Sodaanglobal